A gift for

. . . .

From

. . . .

On this date

. . . .

The Single Woman ™

LIFE, LOVE, AND A
DASH OF SASS

MANDY HALE

THOMAS NELSON
Since 1798

NASHVILLE   DALLAS   MEXICO CITY   RIO DE JANEIRO

Published in Nashville, Tennessee, by Thomas Nelson. Thomas Nelson is a registered trademark of Thomas Nelson, Inc.

Thomas Nelson, Inc., titles may be purchased in bulk for educational, business, fund-raising, or sales promotional use. For information, please e-mail SpecialMarkets@ThomasNelson.com.

ISBN 978-1-4003-2231-2

Printed in the U.S.A.

13 14 15 16 17 RRD 10 9 8 7 6 5 4

If I have a better half, it is my family. This book is dedicated to my mom and dad, Terri and Allen Hale, and my sister and brother-in-law, Cher and Kevin King—my support system, my cheerleaders, my best friends.

To my precious grandmother, Nanny, whose love of writing was ingrained in my spirit long before I was even old enough to read and whose fervent prayers have guided the direction of my life.

To my nieces, Emma and Olivia—two sassy single women in training, so smart and funny and unique. I feel certain this will not be the last time you see their names in print.

And to single girls everywhere who are audacious enough to choose Happy—with or without the Ever After—this book is for you.

Contents

Foreword

I started The Single Woman movement in January 2010, not as a New Year's resolution but as a *revolution*. I had just come out of an exponentially bad relationship of almost two years, one of those relationships that you completely lose yourself and your identity in, and finding your new place in the world after it's all over feels much like learning to acclimate to living on another planet. I was thirty years old, I was beginning my life again, and after alienating most of my friends while I was in the relationship (because I didn't want to see the truth mirrored back at me about just how bad the relationship was), I was in desperate need of inspiration, of a mentor, of a BFF. I was ready to spread my wings, fly solo, and really celebrate my singleness, and I was looking for other female voices out there representing the positive, inspirational, joyful side of single life.

Unfortunately, those voices were nowhere to be found.

The bookstores offered hundreds of books celebrating love and marriage and parenthood and dating—books instructing you on how to date a man, land a man, and keep a man, books detailing how to "get anyone to fall in love with you," "get married in less than a year," or even "survive your single life," but not a word about *celebrating* your single life.

I checked my TV screen. Nope, definitely not there. There were shows about battling dozens of other women for the affections of one man (who, by the way, wasn't even that great), shows about dating in the dark, marrying a millionaire, and even winning the heart of a "celebrity." But absolutely not one show celebrated the journey of the single woman. I checked the church, and although Jesus Himself was a single man, even most churches don't really know what to do with their singles. They teach classes on "preparing for marriage," "waiting for marriage," and "praying for marriage," but what about just honoring exactly who you are in *this* moment instead of always prepping for the next phase of life?

Why was everyone treating single life as the prologue to marriage instead of a wildly beautiful adventure all its own?

I had exhausted all my possibilities and *still* couldn't find a voice of hope for single women among all the voices of discouragement, so I decided to become one.

I started a column, which soon led to The Single Woman Twitter page, which almost overnight began to pick up steam, which led to a Facebook page, which led to the creation of a website a year later, which led to an e-book, which led to this book you are holding in your hands right now. As of this moment, The Single Woman message reaches almost a million people across the world every single day.

It seems I wasn't the only one looking for a voice. A lot of you out there don't agree with the version of single life you're seeing portrayed in society and pop culture.

Instead of "single and fabulous," the life of a single woman in her late twenties and beyond is all too often labeled "single and desperate." Instead of viewed as a choice, *single* seems to denote a lack of options. Everyone seems to want to meddle in the life of the woman who refuses to settle: setting her up on endless dates with guys she has no interest in, calling her desperate, lonely, or too picky, or asking, "What's wrong with her?"

I would like to propose that the question we

should be asking is, "What's right with her?" The way I see it, the solitude, bravery, and uncertain path of the modern-day single woman is something to be applauded as bold and courageous and unique, not lauded as sad or pathetic or weak. As single women, and especially for those of us in our late twenties and beyond, we have racked up countless hours celebrating the choices of our married counterparts—helping them shop for wedding dresses, stepping into an endless stream of really bad bridesmaid dresses, elbowing other women out of the way more times than we care to admit to try to catch that elusive bouquet (praying that maybe, just maybe, if we reach out far enough, we'll catch not only the bouquet but also our own dreams of wearing that white dress to Forever). Is it too much to ask, then, to expect society to celebrate *us* and our choices? To throw a festival of fabulousness in *our* honor, to cheer us single women on for being courageous enough to search for ourselves instead of endlessly searching for a mate?

Love is a beautiful, wonderful, and even sacred thing, but until it arrives, shouldn't we give ourselves permission to *thrive*?

The thing that the movies, greeting cards, and your great-aunt Ida (who shoots sympathetic looks your way and slips copies of *The Old Maid's Survival Guide* to you at family gatherings) fail to portray is an accurate picture of the life of the single woman. I don't know about you, but I *like* being able to spend money on myself without asking anyone's permission. I *like* to take myself out on a weekly date to the bookstore or the movies and spend time in my own company. I *like* staying in my pajamas all day long and watching *Friends* reruns while eating a box of Oreos and not feeling guilty about it.

I *like* taking weekend trips on a whim, not having to shave my legs if I don't want to, and blasting Girl Power tunes and singing into the broom handle while I'm cleaning my house. I *like* the freedom that comes with belonging to me and only me, to have and to hold, in sickness and in health, forsaking all others till death do us part. And although I'd love to have someone eventually join me on my journey, I plan to celebrate my life for the party that it is, even if Prince Charming never does RSVP. Isn't it time to flip the script on what society has handed us and start to see ourselves for the truly brave, empowered, sassy women we are?

We are tough. We are bold. We are fierce. We are

forces to be reckoned with. We face the world the single way every single day, and we don't back down. We don't let the idea of going to dinner alone intimidate us. We don't let the threat of bumping into an ex stop us from going to a party with our heads held high. We walk a path that forces us to step out of our comfort zones constantly. It's a path that a majority of the women we grew up with and acted as bridesmaids for will never have to walk. The journey of a single woman is not an easy one, but we welcome the unknown. We embrace our freedom as the gift that it is. We pay our own way, we march to the beat of our own drum, and we ask permission from no one to do so.

There is a fire in the souls of single women that can never quite be tamed. It's an unwillingness to settle, an independence all our own, built from the knowledge that we can do anything we want. We possess a wisdom that comes from surviving many a broken heart, a shine that comes from learning how to make an entrance into a room accompanied by no one but ourselves, and a confidence that comes from knowing we are not afraid to fall. We know that each time we fall, God presents us with another opportunity to get up and move up. We are strong. We are invincible. We are all The Single Woman.

She Is the Single Woman

She might be the bravest woman I know.

She walks the unaccompanied path. She has her own back. She asks for no favors. Not an ounce of independence does she lack.

She has moments when she feels as though no one sees her. She feels people *look* at her, but do they really *see* her? She gets catcalls when she walks down the street, yet she goes to bed alone.

She's not afraid to change her mind but petrified to change a tire. She makes her own decisions but can't make toast without burning it. Her idea of a three-course meal is a Lean Cuisine. Shoes are in her cupboard where flour and sugar are supposed to be.

She's sassy and feisty to those she meets, but some nights her tears fall on empty sheets.

She has moments when she knows that she's

beautiful and moments when she doubts everything about herself.

She screws up—a lot. She stumbles and she falls. She gets it wrong as often as she gets it right. But she never gives up the fight.

She has bad hair days. She'll buy a new dress at Target and hope it passes for something a little fancier. Sometimes she struggles to make her rent and her car payment in the same month. Because she bought too many shoes? Sometimes. But the only pair of designer shoes she has in her collection is a pair of Christian LaCroix that she got half-off at a sidewalk sale.

Sometimes her friends let her down. They don't always say the right things. And the elusive One That Got Away? She has days when she still can't cut the strings.

She has moments of panic when she wonders if her Prince Charming got lost somewhere or decided to settle for another less complicated, less stubborn, less independent princess. Sometimes she doesn't know where she's going until she gets there.

She hasn't got it all figured out . . . far from it, in fact.

But she loves God and she loves to dance, and she's her own better half.

The bravest woman I know?
She is the reason I do what I do.
She is The Single Woman.
She's me. And she's you.

Part One

Happily Single

Happily Single

The Single Woman Says:

Not everything in life has to be about finding The One. Sometimes a girl just wants to have fun.

*B*eing Happily Single doesn't mean you've sworn off love. It doesn't mean you're ready to sign a lifetime oath of singleness, or that you've given up the hope of finding your Happy Ending. It simply means that you're determined to have a Happy Everything. It's recognizing that you don't need or want to be rescued from your life by a handsome prince because your life is pretty awesome as is.

Happily Single is traveling wherever you want, whenever you want. It's doing Zumba around your apartment in your pajamas at midnight and eating ice cream for dinner if the mood strikes. Happily Single is devoting your time to your passions, dreams, and goals without distractions. It's figuring out your path before you join someone else on his. Happily Single is refusing to compromise any part of yourself to fit into a mold someone else created for you. It's having the permission to *choose* your life rather than having it handed to you, and it's living life on your own terms instead of those that are expected of you.

> The *real* fairy tale is designing a life that's so amazing that you don't want to be rescued from it.

Happily Single takes a strength that most women will never know. It's refusing to let your life be defined by your relationship status and instead defining it yourself. It's laughing in the face of stigmas and stereotypes. It's showing the world that for you, settling is not an option.

Happily Single is also the precursor to Happily Taken. You simply can't have one without the other.

Happily Single is holding out for the best and letting go of the rest. It's saying "I will and I can" to yourself before you say "I do" to someone else. It means you're not looking for a better half because you are already whole. And ultimately, it means that someday when you do invite someone to join you on your journey, it will be because he complements your life, not because he completes it.

Alone but Not Lonely

The Single Woman Says:

Being brave enough to be alone
frees you up to invite people into
your life because you want them,
not because you need them.

I've been thinking a lot lately about the word *alone* and how it carries such negative connotations. I decided it might be a good idea to look this word up because so many people seem to have such a problem with being alone. Why not get to the bottom of what's so dreaded about this little five-letter word?

The first definition I found reads: "separate, apart, or isolated from others." Now look closely at the second definition: "unique; unequaled; unexcelled."

Think about that. Many people are so terrified

to be alone that they settle for loveless relationships or stay trapped in miserable ones for months, even years, on end. But as it turns out, *alone* means "unique; unequaled; unexcelled." In other words: Unparalleled. Unrepeatable. Unable to be imitated or duplicated. Brave. Fabulously original.

Before you willingly allow yourself out of desperation to be a party of two, to be locked in a cage that was never meant for you, take a moment to reconsider your options. Ask yourself:

- ♡ Do I really want to settle for a relationship out of loneliness?
- ♡ Can't I still live the life of my dreams, even if it's without the man of my dreams?
- ♡ Should I really let the status of my love life stop me from loving my life?
- ♡ Do I really want to ground myself just because I happen to be flying solo?
- ♡ Do I want to let other people's opinions stop me from bravely charting my own path?

Or do I want to be the woman who might hope to someday find her One and Only . . . but who, in the meantime, boldly walks alone and dares anyone to call her lonely?

Some steps need to be taken alone. It's the only way to really figure out where you need to go and who you need to be.

Single After Thirty— What's with the Panic?

The Single Woman Says:

You don't need a significant other
to lead a significant life.

I recently paused on one of my favorite morning shows just long enough to see a promo for an upcoming story called "The Sooner the Better." The tagline was "New studies show that 90 percent of women's eggs are gone by age thirty." I had to assume the news anchor wasn't referring to the kind of eggs you make an omelet with, so I immediately grabbed the remote and flipped off the TV before some know-it-all "expert" could deliver his message of gloom and doom and perform his last rites on my eggs.

When did being single after age thirty become a war zone of warnings and dangers to avoid? "You better get married soon, or you'll be an old maid." "You better hurry before all the good ones are gone." "New studies show that 90 percent of women's eggs are gone by age thirty."

The only thing we single ladies need to be rescued from is the notion that we need to be rescued.

Why is our singleness being treated like a terrorist threat? It's like, "Green—she's dating someone. Whew! No chance of her winding up alone and desperate." Or, "Yellow—uh-oh, another relationship just bit the dust, and she's the one who ended it. She's thirty-one and choosing to be alone! Transition to old maid considered imminent." Or, "Red—she's thirty-four and not willing to go out and marry the first guy she sees even though her eggs are vanishing quicker than the Rooty Tooty Fresh 'N Fruity meal at

IHOP. She's actually taking her time and waiting for Mr. Right. Danger! Danger!"

I would like to propose that everyone put away the scare tactics and take a closer look at the lives of their over-thirty-and-single counterparts. We might not have Prince Charming kneeling in front of us with a glass slipper, but we can afford to buy our own sassy stilettos and escort ourselves to the ball. We pay our own bills, file our own taxes, change our own oil (or cruise on down to Jiffy Lube on Ladies' Day for a half-price oil change, but you get the point), and make a million little independent choices each day without the support of a significant other. It takes guts, bravery, and heart to walk a mile in a single girl's shoes. And sometimes a fabulous pedicure.

Lately I have been so proud to watch my single friends not only venture outside their comfort zones but completely shatter their comfort zones to live their most fabulous lives. One friend has had a lifelong dream of becoming an actress, so she finally ignored the cautionary tales doled out to her by friends and family and is wholeheartedly pursuing her dream. I have another who recently got on a plane by herself and jetted across the world on a trip to Paris—by herself. And still another friend worked up the courage to overcome her huge fear and ask out a smokin' hot guy at her office. Although these things may not seem like earth-shattering accomplishments, they are bold examples of what life can look like for a woman living life on her own terms.

At the end of the day, the Happily Ever After of a single girl may not look like everyone else's, and maybe we've encountered more Mr. Right Nows than Mr. Rights, but we're not going to give in out of fright and settle for less than the best. So stop with the scare tactics and realize: Not everyone has to ride off into the sunset with a man. Some of us just want a tan.

There Is Nothing Single About a Single Mom

Recently I took my two nieces to a movie by myself. The closest I've come to being a mom is being a babysitter, so I thought it would be a walk in the park. As it turns out, a three-hour adventure with two bouncy, sugar-infused, excitable, curly-haired little girls is anything but a walk in the park. More like a walk in the *dark* of "I don't know what I'm doing!" From wiping noses, to wiping bottoms, to making sure no one ate an entire box of gummy bears while I wasn't looking, to managing to hold two sticky and squirmy little hands while balancing water bottles, backpacks, stuffed animals, and giant bags of popcorn—flying solo with two little baby birds in the nest is no small feat. I walked away from that experience with a renewed respect for moms everywhere, especially single moms.

My sister is not a single mom, and neither was my mom. They've been blessed to have husbands around to help carry the load. Still, after a long day of working, cleaning, cooking, defusing arguments, brushing hair, brushing teeth, bathing, and disciplining, and somehow finding five minutes a day to tend to their own needs, they are often physically and mentally drained. So I can't imagine how much more of a burden single moms must carry around on a daily basis, with the well-being and needs of one or more impressionable, innocent, trusting little people riding squarely on their shoulders.

So to the single moms, I salute you.

You have likely never received a standing ovation, but you deserve one.

You are the silent heroes. You are on the front lines of a long and hard-fought battle to raise strong, intelligent, healthy, moral, productive children. You put your own needs second without even pausing to think about it, and you take the small piece of cake (both literally and figuratively) so your little ones can have the bigger one every time without fail. You don't date anyone who can't handle a package deal because it's no longer just about *you*—you're thinking and living for two (or more). You face a million different challenges every single day, and you don't back down. You never even waver. You cry, but only when no one else can see. You hold the hardest and least-paid job there will ever be, and you do so without complaining. And when push comes to shove, you become a dad out of love.

You are a doctor, a teacher, a nurse, a maid, a cook, a referee, a heroine, a provider, a defender, a protector, a true Superwoman.

Wear your cape proudly.

She has to have four arms, four legs, four eyes, two hearts, and double the love. There is nothing single about a single mom.

The Gift of Loneliness

The Single Woman Says:

A season of loneliness and isolation
is when the caterpillar gets its wings.
Remember that the next time you feel alone.

I recently conducted an informal poll on Twitter to find out the biggest challenge we singles face, and far and away, loneliness won the day. This hurt my heart. I actually sat in my booth at Starbucks and cried. I suppose it's not really a huge shock that this is a major issue for single people. I mean, the human instinct is to be coupled up—to have someone to come home to, to grow old with, to share things with. And at times it can seem as if the single season of life is going to drag on forever and ever. Trust me; I know this. I've watched person after person after person on my Facebook page post pictures of their little ones going off to the first day of school, taking dance class, hitting home runs. I have some friends who have kids going into high school when I have yet to get started on having a family of my own. So I understand loneliness in its purest form.

And although it sometimes hurts and feels unfair that I'm not experiencing all the things many people my age are experiencing right now, guess what? They're not experiencing what *I'm* experiencing either. Never forget that the same is true for you. Every time you glance over at your married friends' lives with a flash of envy, believe me, they're glancing over the fence at yours in the same way. The bottom line is this: You're going to face down a little loneliness. It's just the cross that we single folks have to bear. But if you learn to really sit with that loneliness and embrace it as the gift that it is—an opportunity to get to know yourself, to learn how strong you really are, to depend on no one but yourself for your happiness—you will realize that a little loneliness goes a *long* way in creating a richer, deeper, more vibrant and colorful you.

The thing about our married counterparts is this: they have the husband and the 2.5 kids and the white picket fence, but they don't have what we singles still have—a blank canvas. In a sense, they don't have the chance to color both inside and outside the lines of their lives and boldly embrace not knowing what comes next. In many ways, their lives are decided. Settled. Complete. Predictability is not a bad thing, but neither is the unpredictability of the single journey.

Embrace your singleness, and even the loneliness that comes with it, as the launching pad that it is. It is often in our loneliest times that God speaks the loudest. Plus, there's just something really cool about knowing that your destiny is so big that you're not meant to share it with anyone, at least not yet. So loneliness? Bring it on! In the long run, a big destiny is worth a little loneliness.

Loneliness is
designed to help you
discover who you
are and stop looking
outside yourself
for your worth.

Too Fabulous to Settle

The Single Woman Says:

sin •gle (adjective): too strong, too
smart, and too fabulous to settle

When did our relationship status become symbolic of our status in life? When did someone decide it takes "putting a ring on it" to give a woman value and worth? And when did *single* become synonymous with *desperate*? It seems that although women have had the right to vote for decades, we still get strange looks when we choose *single* over *settling* on the ballots of our own lives.

So, for all my ladies out there who are brave enough to go against the grain and choose what kind of life they're going to lead instead of having it handed to them, this one's for you.

This one's for the girls who believe in love but also believe in themselves. The girls who have looked settling in the eye and walked away. The ones who know their worth better than to accept a life less than the one they deserve. The girls who happen to prefer registering for spin class to registering for china. The ones who know they don't need a ring to sing or a mate to be great. The girls who know that a secure *me* has to come before a healthy *we*.

So how can you be sure you're on the right track?

A Self Checkpoint for the Single Woman

- ♡ Am I complete in my own life, even if no one ever joins me on my journey?
- ♡ Have I built a healthy network of friends and family who love me the way I am, and do I maintain those relationships even when I'm dating someone?
- ♡ Am I ignoring my dreams to pursue a relationship, or am I pursuing my dreams and letting love find me?
- ♡ Have I learned to love myself, even if I choose to be home alone on a Saturday night?

Once you've made sure you're emotionally strong and secure with who you are, you'll come to realize that late-blooming roses are often the sweetest. You'll realize how much you actually like owning your own schedule, your own weekend, your own independence. You will be brave enough to boldly chart your own path, even if it doesn't include a white picket fence. You'll hope for romance, but with or without it you'll crank up the music and dance. And when you look in the mirror, you'll see a woman who doesn't let go of her joy simply because love hasn't yet arrived.

*Singleness is a choice,
not a lack of options.*

The next time you check the box "S" for single, remember this: singleness is no longer a lack of options but a choice—a choice to refuse to let your life be defined by your relationship status and to live every day Happily and let your Ever After work itself out. Whether or not you have someone in the passenger seat, you are still the driver of your own life and can take whatever road you choose. So the next time you hit a speed bump, otherwise known as the age-old question, "Why are you still single?" look 'em in the eye and say, "Because I'm too strong, too smart, and too fabulous to settle."

Part Two

Being You and Loving It

You Have to Know Yourself Before You Can Be Yourself

The Single Woman Says:

Don't be afraid to be who you are, no matter who that person might be.

For a woman making her mark on the world in the modern age, it can be a little puzzling to figure out exactly who she is. Lots of confusing ideas and mixed messages are out there in the world today from the media, pop culture, and societal standards about who we're supposed to be. And all this talk of "being yourself" and "loving yourself" can leave a girl asking, "Just who am I?"

"Finding ourselves" can be especially difficult for single women, as our walk is vastly different from that of our married counterparts. We don't have marriage or kids from which to take our cues. Although we're standing fearlessly alone in our sassiest stilettos, we have to know what exactly it is we're standing *for.* Otherwise, as the old adage says, "If you're not standing for something, you'll fall for anything."

The good news is, single women have the luxury of establishing their own identities without consultation, permission, or input from anyone. And here's the most important thing to remember: you don't *think* your way into finding out who you are; you *live* your way into it. You make mistakes. You follow your passion. You take wrong turns. You set goals and chase dreams. You figure out what makes you laugh, and you do more of it. You learn what makes you cry, and you do less of it. You try out careers, friendships, and hobbies, and you see which ones fit. You move out of your comfort zone. And you don't apologize for your imperfect journey because every step along the way is one step closer to figuring out who you are and why you were put on this earth.

A girl who truly knows herself is a girl everybody else wants to know.

Ultimately, it's vital to stop looking to everyone else for your identity. The answer can only be found in the mirror. Remember, you have a destiny and a purpose no one else on this earth can fulfill, and you have traveled a unique journey that has equipped you with the tools you need to carry it out. And in an ever-changing, ever-evolving world, *you* are your most beautiful constant. So do the work, take the chances, and risk the growing pains that come with discovering who you really are. You'll be introduced to a lot of people in your life, but that moment you come face-to-face with yourself for the very first time might be the most glorious meeting of all.

Maybe It's Not Maybelline

The Single Woman Says:

You've got to love yourself enough to
look inside you and not beside you for
your joy, confidence, and self-worth.

My nose is too big. My teeth are too crooked. My hips are too wide. My hair is too short." All too often the list of things we don't like about ourselves outweighs the list of things we love about ourselves. But here's the good news: God designed every curve of your body, every line on your face, and every hair on your head for a purpose. He made you completely, wholly, entirely special, from head to toe. Isn't that a wondrous, marvelous thought? If you ever doubt that you are heaven-sent, remember that you are as unique as your own fingerprint!

Consider the fact that maybe, just maybe, beauty and worth aren't found in a makeup bottle, a salon-fresh hairstyle, or a fabulous outfit. Maybe our sparkle comes from somewhere deeper inside, somewhere so pure and authentic and real that it doesn't need gloss or polish or glitter to shine.

True beauty isn't about being a size 2. It's about giving the world the best version of you!

When you're tempted to get down on yourself because of the way you look on the outside, remember that your true beauty comes from who you are on the inside. No model, actress, or Miss America contender can outshine a happy, confident, secure woman.

Is loving yourself as you are a permission slip to slack off—to hit Krispy Kreme every time the Hot Now sign is on, to stay up all night watching bad reruns instead of resting, to start an IV drip of Starbucks so the caffeine will get to the right places faster? No! Self-love is about contentment, not complacency. It is important and even vital to your well-being to love yourself and accept all your imperfections and flaws, but it is not okay to hide behind self-love to avoid self-improvement. Part of loving yourself is giving your body the nutrition, rest, and exercise it needs. That way, your self-love on the inside matches your self-love on the outside. Be happy with who you are, but never stop aiming higher, trying harder, reaching further. There is always room for growth!

When you take good care of yourself, your whole self, you can have the courage to accept yourself a little more loudly and love yourself a little more proudly, reveling in your imperfections as the one-of-a-kind trademarks of authenticity they are.

Maybe it's not Maybelline after all. Maybe you *were* just born with it.

It's Called Self-Worth for a Reason

The Single Woman Says:

Self-love, self-respect, self-approval, and self-worth do not equal self-*ish*.

*O*nce, back in high school, my girlfriends and I were excitedly jumping into my best friend's car to head out to a ball game. So many of us were piling into the car that my BFF didn't notice I wasn't in the car before she took off. As a result of our chattering and rushing to get to our destination (because as I'm sure you recall, everything was *so* important and *so* urgent in high school), my scarf ended up in the car while the rest of my body was still outside the slammed door. So for a full ten seconds or so,

I was basically jogging alongside the car, frantically trying not to get yanked off my feet. Thankfully, my friends noticed the crazy screaming girl beating on the windows, and the car screeched to a halt in time to let me in before I became a human streamer, flapping helplessly in the breeze.

My point is this: When you live in shackles to other people's opinions and moods and judgments, it is the equivalent of becoming a human streamer. And you're better than that. You're meant to be in the driver's seat of your life, not running alongside the car, trying to catch up!

Here's a little secret that's going to save you a lot of unnecessary grief in life. Are you ready?

Your worth is not tied to any person.

Life will be a miserable experience if you spend it worrying about others' disapproval rather than letting your light shine without fear. I'm learning that not everyone is meant to understand us, approve of us, or join us on our journeys. Some would slow us. Others would deter us. Some would jump in the car and take off without us! And some are giant roadblocks that would keep us from the destiny God has for us. So trust that the people who strayed from your path don't belong there anyway. Not everybody can go where you're going.

An amazing thing happens when you stop seeking approval and validation: you find it. People are naturally drawn like magnets to those who know who they are and cannot be shaken! Looking to someone else for the things you should be giving yourself only serves to water down the person you were born to be. It is vital to be so rooted in who you are that you're not yanked off your feet by someone else's opinion or disapproval.

The bottom line: the ones who are meant to get you will get you, and the ones who aren't will be mystified by you. And that's okay. It's not your place to try to please everyone or earn everyone's approval. After all, you're not here to fit nicely inside anyone's mold. You're here to break it.

You will never gain anyone's approval by begging for it. When you stand confident in your own worth, respect follows.

Why Liking Yourself Is Just as Important as Loving Yourself

The Single Woman Says:

You cannot ask someone to like you or love you more than you like or love yourself. You have to set the standard.

We talk a lot about the importance of loving ourselves, but what about just simply *liking* ourselves? I have found that you can love someone—an ornery family member, a coworker who has sat in the cubicle next to you forever and knows no other way to talk than with his mouth full, a longtime friend whom you outgrew long ago, but habit keeps you in each other's lives—without liking them very much. Very often, we love out of obligation, but *like* . . . like is a choice. And that's especially true when it comes to liking ourselves.

The importance of liking yourself cannot be underestimated. The bottom line: if you're constantly down on yourself, questioning your worth, and doubtful about the value you bring to this world, others are eventually going to develop the same opinions about you that you have about yourself. Ask yourself a few questions:

How Do I Feel About Me?

♡ Would I hang out with me?
♡ Would I want to be my own best friend?
♡ What makes me a good friend?
♡ What is my best personality trait?
♡ Do I feel not only worthy of love but also worthy of *like*?
♡ What can I do to be kinder to myself?

In this world, you're going to come up against enough faux friends and fair-weather friends. *You* shouldn't be one of them. You have to have your own back! When you are your own best friend, you don't endlessly seek out relationships, friendships, and validation from the wrong sources because you realize that the only approval and validation you need is your own. Find yourself first, like yourself first, love yourself first, and friendship, companionship, and love will naturally find you. Don't just love yourself out of obligation because it seems like the right thing to do. Like yourself out of recognition that there is not, has not been, and will never be another *you*.

You are never really alone if you make friends with the person in the mirror.

Your Self-Worth Is Not for Sale

The Single Woman Says:

Stand strong in your worth, and don't let anyone talk you out of it.

Although I often talk about figuratively "deciding what makes you happy and holding a yard sale for everything that doesn't," actually holding a yard sale is quite handy for learning other valuable life lessons. Recently my family and I held a yard sale, and it really opened my eyes to the parallels between undervaluing your belongings and undervaluing yourself.

For example, one of the items I was selling was a brand-new tutu that I wore only once as part of a

Halloween costume. I bought the tutu for around thirty dollars, and it was in mint condition. I'm extremely familiar with yard sale pricing, so I put a price tag of one dollar on the tutu, thinking it was more than reasonable for a practically new item. Well, one of the yard sale customers picked it up, looked it over, and asked if I would take fifty cents for it because it had "a rip in the lining." (There was no such rip in the lining, by the way.) I promptly told her no, I would not take fifty cents for an essentially brand-new item that I purchased for around thirty dollars. She threw the tutu down and huffed off, and my dad turned to me and asked, "Why didn't you just sell it to her?"

When you start to doubt your worth, remember that God created you like no one else. Very deliberately, He made you you!

Well, to me, the reason was obvious. The item was worth much more than what she was willing to give. I would frankly rather have kept the tutu myself, even if I never wore it again, than sell it for less than what I felt it was worth. And sure enough, a couple of hours later, another lady handed over the one dollar I was asking for the tutu without batting an eye. So the question here is this: If you surrender your self-worth to someone who doesn't see your true value, what happens when someone comes along who wants to give you what you're worth instead of what you'll settle for?

The bottom line: You've got to know your worth, at yard sales and in life, because a lot of people are going to try to talk you out of it. If they can't see your value, let 'em keep on movin'! Someone out there is looking for exactly what you've got and will never try to undercut your value or question your worth. Some things in life just can't be bartered over or placed on the sale rack, and your self-worth is at the top of the list.

Part Three

Living Your Best Life

Living Your Best Life

The Single Woman Says:

Here's a glorious thought: You don't have to settle. Ever. In love or in life.

Although the bookstores are filled with books telling us how to be happy, how to find love, how to be our best selves, and how to live our best lives, the only true way to live your best life is to refuse to settle for anything less than your best life. There are so many ways to cut corners in today's world. Instead of baking our food, we microwave it. Instead of using diet and exercise to lose weight, we turn to plastic surgery. Instead of "till death do us part," we have seventy-two-day marriages. We have drive-through restaurants, drive-through markets, even drive-through wedding chapels! Everything is done so rapidly; sometimes we forget that a quality life wasn't built in a day. If you want your life to be a five-star reality, you have to stop settling for a fast-food mentality!

When you refuse to settle for less than the best, the best tends to track you down.

When I first graduated from college with a journalism degree, everyone told me to look for a "practical, safe job." Since I was a little girl, my dream was to work in television. I always had stars in my eyes and my head in the clouds, truly believing I could do anything I wanted. I worked as a leasing consultant at an apartment complex for more than a year and a half while I looked for a TV job because I refused to settle for less than the life of my dreams. Meanwhile, everyone around me told me I needed to "get serious," "be reasonable," and settle for a comfortable, safe, "normal" job that would pay the bills and allow me to get by.

I'm here to tell you, "just getting by" isn't enough when you know you were born to shoot for the sky.

After months of determination, I secured a job at the local ABC affiliate in Nashville as an associate producer and then moved on to Country Music Television (CMT) as a producer. And although I only ended up working in television for about three years before switching to public relations, I got to live my dream. And I did so because I flatly refused to listen to the voices around me urging me to settle for the mundane, average, and ordinary. I knew I was meant for something extraordinary.

My point is this: refuse to lower your standards, your aspirations, and your expectations for any reason. We were not put here on this earth to barely squeak by and settle for a lukewarm, watered-down version of life, or to live in fear of what other people will think. Our lives can't rise any higher than our standards. Rise above settling in life or in love. And next time someone tells you your standards are too high, don't apologize. Tell them, "Thank you." The standards you set determine the life you get. And those who know their worth don't even entertain the lesser things. They hold out for the best things.

Living in the Now

The Single Woman Says:

When you live in the present, the past is
forgotten and the future takes care of itself.

Hanging out in the past might feel cozy, comfortable, and safe to you, but it's really the riskiest thing
you can do. If you've been there, done that, and gotten the T-shirt, isn't it time to move on to a new
destination? Don't waste a lot of time stressing the
"could haves" because if it should have, it would have!
Realize that everything that has happened in your
life up until now was part of the design to get you
where you're meant to be. When you stare at what's
behind you, you miss out on all the amazing, fabulous things that are right in front of you. And what

you have in store is so much better than anything that has come before!

To get over the past, you first have to accept that the past is over.

My Top Five Ways to Move Past the Past

- ♡ Put away all memorabilia that reminds you of that person, that job, that bad decision that is best forgotten. Photos, e-mails, gifts, phone contacts, whatever it takes.
- ♡ Ask a friend to hold you accountable, to stop you when you talk about that past regret or ex or really bad decision. I once tried snapping a rubber band on my wrist to literally "slap myself on the wrist" every time I thought about an ex. I don't recommend this. Go with a friend instead. It's the kinder, gentler option.
- ♡ Get involved in something new and exciting. The hobby you always wanted to try, the trip you always wanted to take, the degree you always meant to get. Dream big.
- ♡ Create a Vision Board with all your dreams and goals listed in one place. Then check them off, one by one, as you let your present successes erase your past messes.

♡ Contribute to the greater good by volunteering for a cause that's near and dear to your heart. Put all that sweatin' you're doing over the things you can't change behind someone or something that you *can* change!

No matter how many times you revisit it, analyze it, regret it, or sweat it, the past is over. It can hurt you no more. When you start to accept the past and everything that took place there as events that happened *for* you and not *to* you, life will open up to you in remarkable ways. So go ahead. Stop glancing at what was, and start dancing with what is!

The past may be more certain than the future because it's already happened, but you will most certainly never get anywhere you're meant to go by traveling yesterday's road. Embrace the delightful unknown of the here and now, and watch your world come to life! Stop trying to skip ahead to the next chapter or flip back to the last chapter, and enjoy the page you're on right this very minute. We can't ever know what's going to happen next, but isn't that half the fun of life?

There is beauty and magic and power in the *now*. Realize that you've outgrown your past and it's time to <u>let it go</u>. Look upon where you've been as merely the prologue to the epic story that is your life. The best gift you will ever give yourself is living fully in the present. The future might be a little too loose and the past a little too tight, but the present fits just right.

No matter how much you stress or obsess about the past or future, you can't change either one. In the present is where your power lies.

Happiness Kicks "Buts"

The Single Woman Says:

Happiness doesn't have to be chased.
It merely has to be chosen.

"If I can only lose five pounds, I'll be happy."

"If I get this job promotion, I'll be happy."

"If the person I like asks me out, I'll be happy."

"But I don't have the life of my dreams yet."

"But I still have so far to go."

"But he hurt me and broke my heart."

We can literally "if" and "but" ourselves right out of happiness! The truth of the matter is, no faraway, distant, magical future is going to suddenly flip the switch on our happiness. There is only here and now. This moment. This day. This hour. Your beautiful, wonderful, fantastical life is staring you in the face, waiting for you to stop wishing it away and start living it. Sometimes we treat happiness like that kid in gym class who always gets picked last for the kickball team (and I know because I was always that kid). We choose fear first, we choose self-pity first, we choose misery first, we choose unforgiveness first . . . but the only way we're ever going to kick the "buts" right out of our lives is if we ardently, passionately, exuberantly choose happiness!

You're up. It's your turn to pick teams. Will you go on debating, waiting, and hesitating, or will you choose this moment to make happiness your number one draft pick? Often in life we get so caught up in what we don't have that we forget to be grateful for what we do have. We get so busy asking and seeking and begging and pursuing that we never take time out simply to be. To sit still and contemplate just how marvelous life really is, and how blessed we are to be a part of it. Wherever you are in your journey, take a minute to stop and give thanks for life. For love. For family. For faith. For friends. For another day. For the chance to get it right, no matter how many times you've gotten it wrong before. No matter what you think you're lacking today, there is so much to be thankful for . . . so much beauty and hope and magic and opportunity and life right in front of you. Don't let another second pass you by without pausing to appreciate it.

Your circumstances cannot control you as long as you choose happiness on the inside, regardless of what's happening on the outside.

Change Your Thoughts, and Your Life Will Follow

The Single Woman Says:

A positive attitude turns "I can't" and
"I won't" into "I have" and "I will."

So many people go through life with their heads hanging down, feeling bad about themselves and their lives, wondering why things never seem to look up for them. There's no big mystery here. In fact, I can crack the code for you right now: your life can't look up until you do! If your life is a mirror and you don't like what you're seeing, change who you're being. Sitting around passively complaining about life will not only fail to make your life better, but it will also make it worse. By focusing on what you don't want, you invite those very things into your life. The Bible says, "As [a man] thinks in his heart, so is he" (Proverbs 23:7). Consider that for a moment. Your thoughts are powerful—whether you succeed or fail is determined in your mind long before it plays out in real time.

The first step to making big, positive changes in your life and flipping the script on those negative thoughts is to realize that you are worthy, you are complete, and you were created just as you are for a purpose that only you can fulfill. Sit down and make a list of ten things you love about yourself. Then repeat those things every morning as your daily affirmations. Here are a few affirmations to get you started!

- ♡ I love myself just as I am.
- ♡ I have a special, one-of-a-kind, God-given destiny.
- ♡ Today I will take active steps to follow my dreams.
- ♡ I will walk by faith and not by sight.
- ♡ I will project positive, loving thoughts to

those around me, even to those who have hurt me.

♡ I have everything I need to fulfill my unique purpose.

♡ My every step is ordered.

♡ I greet the day with confidence, peace, and joy.

♡ I am a whole, healthy person. Any relationship I add to my life will be to complement me, not complete me.

♡ Every day, in every way, I am getting better and better!

Now add your own affirmations to this list, and spend time each day reminding yourself of all the great things about you. Take active steps to boost your self-esteem, and your life will follow. Your thoughts are like a magnet; they determine what you attract. So if you want to live in abundance, stop focusing on what you lack!

By changing your mindset and your attitude, you might just change your life.

Remember, nothing changes if nothing changes. The only thing standing between you and happiness is your thought life—not a better job, a different car, longer hair, or the perfect boyfriend. Even if someone handed you all those things on a silver platter, if you have a bad attitude, you won't appreciate them. Nothing can make you happy until you make yourself happy. And nothing is ever going to be enough for you until you realize that you are enough.

If you are alive and well today, you are already infinitely more blessed than scores of people around the globe. Take a good look around and realize how much you have to be grateful for. Then start giving the world your thanks instead of your complaints. Your altitude changes when your attitude changes! The formula for success really is as simple as this: change your thoughts = change your life.

Playing It Safe Is the Riskiest Thing You Can Do

The Single Woman Says:

To truly live, we must be willing to take risks.

It's easy to get stuck in a rut of what we think we *should* be doing instead of going after what we *dream* of doing. We play it safe just to stay in the game. We put our own dreams on hold to answer someone else's phone. We stay in the "comfortable" relationship and forgo meeting our real soulmate, or we delay a destiny that can only be realized by flying solo, all because we're too scared to be alone. We avoid the unknown and stay firmly planted in our comfort zone. We don't move to the big city, we don't write that book we always dreamed of writing, or we don't pursue a particular career because it's not "practical" enough. All the while, we let precious time we could have spent pursuing our passions, chasing our goals, and living the lives of our dreams slip away. We spend so much time trying to set "realistic" goals that we never live up to the full potential of who we are as human beings. We instead resign ourselves to living easy, ordinary, mundane lives spent "playing by the rules" and coloring inside the lines.

Sometimes in life you have to risk everything you've got to get everything you ever wanted.

Life isn't about the length of your stay here on earth. It's about what you do with the time you *do* have. It's about refusing to live a life inside the box. It's about deciding right now, this minute, that "good enough" is not good enough and you are going to give the world your very best. It's about knowing so strongly that you were born to fly that you're willing to leap off the edge and grow your wings on the way down. It's about challenging the status quo. It's about going a little further, trying a little harder, reaching a little higher. Life is too short, too fleeting, and too brief to do anything less than what you love to do.

Playing it safe is the riskiest thing you can do. The price you pay for allowing life to pass you by is just too high! Take some time to evaluate your life and ask yourself, *Am I giving everything I can to the pursuit of my dreams?* Then realize it's later than it seems. Anything in your life that's acting as a security blanket is only smothering the person you were born to be. Toss it out the window and be free!

The Sweetness of the Surrendered Life

The other night I was relaxing (or so I thought!) in my bed watching a movie when I suddenly became aware of my posture. Although it was late, quiet, and peaceful in my little apartment and I had no deadlines or stressors pressing down on me, my shoulders were hunched up in a tight ball of tension, and my abs were clenched as if I were poised for battle. When I had this moment of clarity and paid attention to what my body was telling me, it truly surprised me. Most of us go through life on autopilot, and we don't ever really stop to see what our bodies are telling us. Mine was telling me, quite simply, "Mandy, you don't know how to relax." Since that night, I have begun to do little check-ins with myself throughout the day, and I've found that I've adopted the same tense, rigid stance in many other scenarios. When I'm driving my car, for example, I tend to hunch over the steering wheel, all tied up in bundles of stress.

So what has us all on edge? As a society, we go through life holding our breath, waiting for the other shoe to drop. Anxiety is at an all-time high as we deal with threats of terror alerts, unemployment rates, soaring gas prices, deadlines, obligations, and traffic jams. We spend so much time trying to put out fires that we never have a chance simply to relax in front of them. But what can we do about it? Isn't that "just life"?

The things we don't stress tend to turn out best. Trust and let go.

In a word, no. Being a constant bundle of nerves, tension, and anxiety is not "just life." It's waiting to live and living in fear; it's not actually living.

Simple Ways to De-stress

- ♡ Exercise! You don't have to go all P90X or anything. A simple walk around the block can work wonders! And exercising not only helps you relax, but it also releases endorphins, which make you feel happy. Plus, it offers the added bonus of getting you a little closer to those skinny jeans in the top of your closet you wondered if you'd ever get to wear again.
- ♡ Pamper yourself. Get a massage or a mani/pedi, take a bubble bath, go buy that pair of shoes you've been eyeballing for a month. A big cause of stress is forgetting to take care of yourself. Sometimes a little "vitamin TLC" is just what the doctor ordered.
- ♡ Talk to a friend, or pray. Your friends are always there to listen. So is God.
- ♡ Journal. Sometimes just putting what you're feeling into writing is enough to release the burden and make you feel lighter.
- ♡ Channel all that energy into something

creative. Take a dance class. Paint a picture. Finally start that Pinterest project of turning old candle jars into snow globes.

Stress is energy that needs to be released, so instead of letting it work against you, make it work *for* you!

Sometimes it's okay just to let go, relax into life, float, and let God carry you, trusting that He is the ultimate life raft. If you were swimming, you wouldn't try to grasp tightly to the water to stay afloat, would you? No, you would let go and relax into the ocean's waves. So why do we find this so hard to do in life? Pay attention, even now, to how you're sitting as you're reading this. Are your shoulders bunched up and tight? Is your neck stiff? Are your abs clenched as if you're waiting to go to battle? Then stop. Breathe. Exhale. Relax. Trust. Stop holding your breath, and allow life to take your breath away. You can surrender. You can let go. Will everything turn out exactly as you hope or plan? No. Not everything. That's just part of life. But then again, some things will turn out even better! And either way it goes, the best approach is to truly believe that whatever happens, God is in control.

Part Four

Matters of the
Heart: Love, Dating,
and Friendships

Love Is Worth the Risk

Love is patient, love is kind. It does not envy, it does not boast, it is not proud. It does not dishonor others, it is not self-seeking, it is not easily angered, it keeps no record of wrongs. Love does not delight in evil but rejoices with the truth. It always protects, always trusts, always hopes, always perseveres.

—1 Corinthians 13:4–7 NIV

One of the number one issues at the forefront of a single woman's mind is—you guessed it—love. *When am I going to find it? Am I going to find it? Is there one person out there for everyone? Have I ever really been in love?* Love is defined in many ways. Ask people on the street for their definition of love, and you'll get no two answers the same. The Bible defines love. Movies define love. Turn on the radio, and you'll get another definition of love. We see evidence of love in the unlikeliest of places and among the unlikeliest of men and women. Your cat loves you. Your dog loves you. Your neighbor loves you. Your mom loves you. Love is everywhere we look. It makes the world go round, you know.

But you can't always follow the definitions of others, "the rules," or even the advice of the most renowned experts when it comes to matters of the heart. It's easy to write about love. It's another thing altogether to experience love. And although I am a big believer in fairy tales and happy endings, I'm not all that sure how accurate Hollywood's portrayal of love is. I've definitely had my share of "movie moments" in my day, but I've found that the most poignant expressions of love are found not in the grand gestures but in the quiet moments. Sharing a laugh or a milkshake. Finishing each other's sentences.

I once had a guy *shut down a jewelry store in New York City for me* to show me massively huge engagement rings. But at the end of the day, he didn't propose. And you know what meant more to me? The simple note my high school sweetheart had left on my windshield during our senior year, telling me to have a good day. Why? Because the New York City experience sure glittered a lot, but it wasn't gold. The note, on the other hand, was and still is more precious to me than any diamond because it was *real* and pure and came from the heart.

There's a lot I still don't know about love, but let me tell you what I do know. Regardless of how it ends, love is always worth going out on a limb for. Better to put your heart on the line and walk away with nothing than to play it safe.

Love often doesn't make any sense at all. It likes to creep up on you when you're least expecting it, with the person you're least expecting it to be with. It climbs walls and crosses oceans to find you. When it's your time, love will track you down.

Love isn't possession, it isn't codependency, it isn't jealousy, and it isn't neediness or clinginess. It's not meant to complete you, but to complement you. If it's toxic, it isn't love. Love isn't finding a "better half," but an "equal match." Love is letting go when you want to hold on. Love will never require you to sacrifice your dreams or your dignity.

Love isn't uncertainty. It isn't a "maybe" thing. It isn't a question. It's always an answer.

Love is beautiful. It is magical. It is life-changing. It is breathtaking.

So hope for love, pray for love, wish for love, dream for love . . . but don't put your life on hold waiting for love. Until it arrives, give yourself permission to thrive! Happy is still Happy, with or without the Ever After.

Love is a lot of things, but "safe" isn't one of them. It's always a risk to love. But it's a bigger risk not to.

Love Moves Mountains—It Doesn't Straddle Fences

The Single Woman Says:

The right one for you will move mountains to be with you. He won't hide behind them.

I get a lot of questions from ladies—beautiful, amazing, worthy, successful, got-it-going-on ladies—to the effect of, "If he's not calling me, what does that mean?" "We went out once and he never asked me out again. Do you think he's just shy?" "He wants to sleep with me, but he doesn't want to date me. Do you think he cares about me?"

It makes my heart hurt to see these fierce, fabulous females so twisted up inside about guys who don't even deserve a second glance, let alone a third, fourth, or fifth chance. In no way am I male-bashing or man-hating, but the cold, hard truth is: if a man wants to be with you, he will make his actions clear. There won't be any questions, murkiness, cloudiness, or fear.

The Right Man . . .

- ♡ will have time for you.
- ♡ will not be intimidated by you or scared of commitment.
- ♡ will be entirely single—not married or otherwise spoken for.
- ♡ will not expect to sleep with you just because he's dating you.
- ♡ will be interested in a relationship, not a hookup. And he'll know the difference.
- ♡ will respect your morals and beliefs.

Typically, if a man is into you, you won't even have to question his feelings because they will be crystal clear. The truth is, people, and men in particular, dread confrontation. They avoid it like the plague. They will hand you any excuse in the world to get out of handing you the truth—that they're just not really feeling it. So it's up to us as women, being the intuitive creatures that we are, to read between the lines of their hesitation and indecision and figure out that if he's not pursuing us and initiating contact with us—he's not calling us, texting us, Facebooking us, tweeting us, IM'ing us, or asking us out—then (*dum da da dum*) he's probably not the person we're meant to be with. After all, dating isn't supposed to be like a game of *Where's Waldo?*

> *Love shouldn't require Windex to be clear. It either is or it isn't.*

Think about it: If you have to chase a man or convince him why he should be with you, do you really want to be with him? You are far too fabulous to beg, crawl, manipulate, or convince. It's time to write yourself a big ole reality check and keep the change. Let go of that dead-end relationship and hit the highway to Loving Yourself Too Much to Wait Around for Someone Who Doesn't Love You Enough. Someone out there will be so excited, thrilled, and honored to call you his girl that he would never string you along. But you'll never meet him as long as you're clinging to Mr. Wrong.

Do you know the wonderful, beautiful thing that happens when you rid yourself of people who don't see your worth? You make space in your life for all the glorious people you deserve. And I can't think of a better Hollywood ending than that.

Don't Play Hard to Get—Be Hard to Get

The Single Woman Says:

Too easy to get = Just as easy to forget.

Picture it: You pick up the phone to call your new crush for the very first time. You know the drill—your heart is racing, your blood is pumping, and you can hardly wait for him to answer. One ring . . . two rings . . . three rings . . . voice mail. You leave a message (the perfect, breezy message), just knowing that you'll hear back from him in no time. Two hours go by and still nothing. It can't hurt to shoot him a quick text, right? Maybe he didn't get your voice mail. Maybe his voice mail is broken! Maybe there's a glitch with the cell tower three towns over that's causing his voice mail to delete all messages spontaneously. So you shoot him the perfect, breezy text . . . and still nothing. You text your best friend to see if maybe your text messaging is malfunctioning (c'mon, ladies, we've all done it), but it's not. You call your cell phone provider to tell them, "Mr. Telephone Man, there's something wrong with my line," only to be told that not only is cell service working, but they've actually installed three new towers in your crush's backyard in the past week and he now has the capacity to make a call without even picking up the phone. You realize you have no other choice but to take drastic action and perform CPR on your phone to bring it back to life, when—*Brrring!* Your phone lights up! A call! You answer excitedly, only to be told by an automated telemarketer, "Please hold for an important message." *Sigh.* What went wrong? What happened to make Mr. Wonderful suddenly shadier than a pool umbrella on a hot summer day?

Chances are, you made yourself too available to him. Since ancient times, man has thrived on the thrill of the hunt, the excitement of the pursuit, and if you make it too easy on him, he feels deprived of the chance to win your affections. He wants to be able to steal your heart and earn your love. Set your affections, your heart, and your precious time out on the doorstep without so much as making him ring the doorbell first, and he'll treat you like a doormat. Make him work a little to get next to you, and he won't stop till you're his.

Am I suggesting you play games? Not at all. I'm not suggesting you "pretend" to have a life; I'm suggesting you actually go out and get one. A busy, vibrant, goal-oriented woman is so much more attractive than a woman who waits around for a man to validate her existence. You have a fabulous, busy, rewarding life of your own, so don't always be so quick to leave yours and go rushing over to his! A woman who's not afraid to be unpredictable is a woman who will always keep his attention.

The bottom line: love yourself enough to pursue your own dreams and your own passions in such a way that you will never be mistaken for a girl without a life and a mind of her own. Don't make your crush the center of your universe; make him a fantastic constellation that you gaze at and enjoy from time to time but that doesn't stop your world from spinning happily on its axis. Your value and your worth are never going to be wrapped up in another human being. The only person you have to live with every day for the rest of your life is yourself, so start with making her happy, and the rest will fall into place.

Be a bit of a
challenge, not
because you're
playing games
but because you
realize you're worth
the extra effort.

Relationship Red Flags: When to Slow and When to Go

Red flags. They're those annoying yet necessary little touchstones in life that guide us not toward but away from things. They're the subtle prods from God that something's not right, those gut feelings that you can't quite put your finger on. Yes, red flags along our journeys are very real, and whether we choose to heed them or ignore them determines where we end up.

Although red flags can warn us against making the wrong decisions in virtually any area of our lives, perhaps the most commonly misread red flag is the relationship red flag. We find someone we like and who likes us, and although we might have a tiny sense of unease that something isn't quite right, we forge ahead, thinking we're just imagining things and overreacting. Before we know it, our tiny sense of unease turns into foreboding, our foreboding into sheer dread, and then we find ourselves careening full steam ahead toward the crash of all crashes, simply because we didn't heed that still, small voice the first time it spoke up. When we run through a stop sign, what happens? Danger. Calamity. Chaos. Injury, to our person or to our emotions. So why do we stubbornly barrel toward a relationship that's not meant for us when our intuition is telling us otherwise?

Maybe someone shows a slight hint of a temper on your first date; he yells at the waiter because his burger is medium well instead of medium rare. Or maybe, like in one of my most bizarre first dates, the guy asks you for money at the end of the night. This was a guy who seemed perfectly normal. Throughout the entire date, he was so sweet and such a gentleman that I was practically swooning. And then we got to the end of the night. He took both my hands in his, looked deep into my eyes . . . and asked me for forty dollars. Yes. That actually happened. And even though he made up a litany of excuses for why he needed the money and why he couldn't come up with it himself, it was pretty much the sketchiest move in first-date history.

Maybe your red flag isn't as glaring as mine was, but whatever the case may be, if you are feeling even a moment's hesitation, pause and evaluate the situation. Here's a hint: if you ever find yourself asking, *Is God trying to tell me something?* the answer is almost always yes. God sends small rainstorms before He sends flash floods and small detours before roadblocks. A red flag is just a stop sign waiting to happen, signaling a road that you're not meant to go down. God has our backs enough to send the signs, but it's up to us to read them. It takes only one stop sign for us to stop our cars. Why does it take multiple red flags for us to halt a relationship?

Our hearts know what our minds can't yet begin to comprehend. If something on the inside is telling you that someone isn't right for you, he's not right for you, no matter how great he might look on paper. When it's right for you, you will know. And when it's not, it's time to go. Your gut, your instincts, and your intuition inherently know when to proceed with caution or to stop entirely. So listen up when you hear that still, small voice. Even a slight hesitation is reason enough to ask yourself if you need to continue down the road you're on or turn back. Ultimately, red flags are moments of hesitation that determine our destination.

A red flag is just a stop sign waiting to happen.

Honor Your Inner Circle

The Single Woman Says:

Our friends have a way of reminding us of how fabulous we are when the rest of the world has forgotten.

I am thoroughly convinced that some people in this world are just meant to be our friends. Something magical happens the moment you meet, and it strikes a chord across time and space. And it doesn't matter if you met the person two weeks or two months or two years ago, or if you're in the same city or miles apart, because somewhere along the way, when no one was looking, you became not just friends but family. The kind of family who, when the chips are down, reminds you what's really important. The kind of family who makes you laugh until you cry and allows you to cry until you laugh. This kind of friendship is always worth the time, the risk, the silly fights, and the sleepless nights you put into it.

The thing I have learned in a big way recently is the importance of an inner circle. All of us at times have mistaken people who *say* they have our backs for people who really have our backs. Words and actions are two very different things. The people who are there for the good times are great, but the people who are there for the bad times are better. It is vital to realize the difference between friends and onlookers in your life. Onlookers will rush to join you in the limo; real friends will rush to your aid when the limo breaks down. Onlookers will see a brief snapshot of your life and think they know the "real" you; real friends will keep a scrapbook of both your bad and good moments and will love you through both. Onlookers will line up to benefit from your favor and influence; real friends know what it took to get you there. In short, let the onlookers do what they're there to do: look. Then celebrate the people in your life who are there because they love you for no other reason than because you are you.

At the end of the day, it's not the quantity of your tribe but the quality of your tribe that matters. After all, if we all wore diamonds on every finger, it would take away from the rarity and preciousness of the jewel. True, pure, loyal friendship is as rare and precious as diamonds and should be treated as such. It only takes a brief run-in with a cubic zirconia to remember that!

I urge you to take an inventory of your friendships. It won't take much time or energy to ascertain which ones exist only at a surface level and which ones are made of true substance.

A Friendship Inventory

- ♡ If social media and texting and e-mail went away, would your friendships still exist? Are you carrying out entire friendships via Twitter or Facebook? Would you hang out with these people in "real life"?
- ♡ Do you and your closest friends share a whole tapestry of common goals and dreams and passions rather than just one thread? The thing I love so much about my three

closest friends is that we share the common desire not to settle. In any area of our lives. Although we are all at different stages in our lives—Alli is in her early twenties, Jamie is thirty, and Laura is in her early forties—we share the commonality of high standards at any age!

♡ Do the friends in your life inspire you to be better, aim higher, dream bigger? Or do they enable you to stay complacent and stagnant? Do they encourage you and motivate you, or do they discourage you and tear you down? Are their lives something you would aspire to . . . or run from?

♡ How do your friends react when you experience success or when you decide to do something to better yourself? Do they celebrate your choices and victories or mock them?

♡ Do your friends encourage you to be your best but still love you at your worst? People who truly belong in your tribe will allow you to have a bad day, get it wrong, make bad decisions . . . and still love you right through it all. They won't discount months or years of a friendship because of a few bad days.

Now take a moment to honor, celebrate, and give thanks to those who belong in your tribe. They will motivate you, encourage you, challenge you, push you, and be there waiting to catch you if you fall. They're the reason you can take the really big leaps in life because they'll be the ones rooting for you from the ground as you scream all the way down! If life is like a skydiving excursion, then your tribe is your safety net.

Go ahead. Jump.

True friends make
the bad times good
and the good times
unforgettable.

The Evolution of Friendship

The Single Woman Says:

Life changes. Let it.

Single women can sometimes find it difficult to maintain a consistent group of close friends. Our friends change, move away, and (the most common roadblock) get married. Although I have numerous married friends, it can sometimes be a struggle to maintain a close bond with them. First of all, they always seem to want to bring their significant others along anytime we hang out, and when this happens, it's almost impossible not to feel like a fifth wheel. There also seems to be a lack of things to talk about among singles and takens. The common ground between us seems to shrink smaller and smaller with each passing year.

And of course, there's the famous Pity Party that married people like to throw for single people, even when we don't RSVP. They give us looks of sympathy over dinner and patronizing pats on the head. They say, "Don't worry! You'll find someone soon!" Or, "It's not like you're an old maid or anything (yet)." They glance at one another knowingly when you dare to protest and tell them you're happy just as you are. And they attempt to set you up with their coworker's sister's boyfriend's friend, even though you have nothing whatsoever in common except your relationship status.

> Friendships grow and evolve. Just like everything else in life, they're not meant to stay the same.

At the end of the day, whether we're married, single, coupled up, dating, divorced, or whatever the case may be, we're not all that different. We all wish, dream, hope, and plan—yes, perhaps for different things—but we are all in this thing together. Our married friends might be wishing for babies while we're wishing for love. Two very different wishes, two very different places in our lives, but several common denominators: We're all reaching for something bigger. We all hurt. We all face disappointments. We all have great tragedy and equal triumph. We all want to make our marks on the universe, whether it happens by falling in love or by extending that love through bringing a new life into the world.

Instead of calling an end to the friendship because your lives have gone in two different directions, look for ways to merge the two paths. Instead of scoffing at your married friends when they post seventeen pictures of their toddlers on Instagram, or getting frustrated when they cancel plans for the second week in a row because the washing machine broke, show them a little understanding. Realize that they're traveling a new and often scary road that doesn't come with a map, and some days they're probably doing their level best just to muddle their way through. Your acts of kindness and compassion might just inspire your married friends to reach back into their memories of their single days with a little more empathy, remembering that singles are traveling a road that's sometimes harder, rockier, and lonelier than they might want to admit.

Surely if the stars can coexist in the sky, we single and married folks can find a way to coexist together here on earth. And maybe not just coexist but also share a few laughs along the way.

Seasonal Friendships

The Single Woman Says:

You will evolve past certain
people. Let yourself.

*Y*ou may never know why some people pass through your life. Some are there to stay; others are there to show you the way. Some are there to hurt you and in the process show you how strong you really are. Some are there to help you, in ways you might not even realize, until they are long gone from your life. Some are there for a short time simply to introduce you to other people who are meant to stick around for a long time. And some you can't shake no matter how hard you both try. Some are lifetime, and some are seasonal, and it's important to respect the duration of the friendship, no matter how long or short it may be.

The truth is, it happens as we get older and grow up and change: friendships we thought would be in our lives forever turn out to have expiration dates. Your lives are on two separate tracks, and you see no way of going back. And as much as you love her and cherish the memories you've shared together, you know in your heart that the friendship has run its course.

How to Know If a Friendship Is Past Its Prime

- ♡ Your friend is overwhelmingly emotionally needy and draining you of your time and energy.
- ♡ She lied to you, betrayed you, or inflicted some other pain upon you.
- ♡ Your friend is incredibly negative, cynical, and pessimistic and works overtime to rain on your parade because she's jealous of your sun and tired of her shade.
- ♡ You've recently made big, positive changes in your life, and instead of celebrating them, your friend is hating them.
- ♡ No matter what you accomplish or what

incredible, life-changing blessing comes your way, this friend manages to find something wrong with it.

If a particular person in your life is repeatedly choosing not to honor you and is causing you more sadness or pain than joy, it might be time to release that friendship back to God and trust that it is not where you belong. I have had to cut ties with people whom I loved very deeply because they were choosing to abuse the boundaries of our friendship and take advantage of my heart in a way that was causing me great pain. Life is too short for that!

A few years ago I had just started dating my trainer at the gym. Trainer Guy also worked out with a close friend of mine, whom we'll call Violet (to protect the not-so-innocent). Somewhere along the way, I picked up on a vibe that was, for lack of a better word, icky. Uneasy. Like a black cloud hanging over me every time I saw Trainer Guy and Violet. Violet was married, and I had no reason to suspect that anything was going on between her and Trainer Guy, and yet something wasn't right. It was driving me crazy. I confronted Violet; she flatly denied it. I asked her about it again. Denial again.

Violet's behavior over the next few weeks

continued to become more and more odd—evasive even. Things came to a head when I caught her lying to me about going out of town on a business trip. Through a mutual friend, I discovered Violet had actually been in town the entire time. Ultimately, I had to completely sever the friendship. She told me I was crazy. She couldn't believe I would accuse her of such a thing and that one day I would learn the truth and feel foolish.

Guess what? I *did* learn the truth, but it wasn't me who felt foolish. As it turned out, denial *is* just a river in Egypt because a few months later Violet was divorced and another trainer at the gym confided in me that Violet and Trainer Guy had been sneaking around behind my back the entire time.

Sometimes it happens that way. We walk away from a friendship that feels wrong for reasons we can't quite put our finger on, only to find out later that we were right all along.

It hurts to let go of a friendship that means a great deal to you; however, I have found time and again that when you release your hold on a negative friendship (or, as I call it, a "toxic friendship"), God has a way of bringing two or three positive friendships into your life as replacements. We must let go of the old to receive the new; it is a rule of life. Better to hurt temporarily and let go of the negative than to hurt over and over and over again. True friends will love you, support you, honor you, and never trample on the beauty of your friendship by purposely causing you pain. Better to have two or three true friends than rooms full of faux friends.

You can love your friends, forgive them, and want good things for them while moving on without them. The friendship had significance, meaning, and importance for a season. And that season has passed. Just like you wouldn't wear a bikini in the winter or snow boots in the summer, it makes no sense to try to extend a friendship for a lifetime if it was only meant to last a season.

Don't pour a lifetime of effort into a seasonal relationship. Not everyone from the pilot belongs in the finale.

Part Five

Letting Go and
Moving On

The Gift of Good-bye

The Single Woman Says:

You may not see it now, but there is a gift in every good-bye. It takes a good-bye to usher in the next era of life.

Sometimes it's a person who exits our lives for seemingly no reason. Sometimes it's a job, an opportunity, or a dream—the thing we wanted so badly, planned for, hoped for, and prayed for goes up in smoke. Sometimes we get fired when we've been model employees. Sometimes a person we have loved and invested our time, energy, affection, and trust in walks away and leaves us in the dust with little to no explanation.

Here's what I'm here to tell you: Stop trying to

solve the mystery. Stop banging your head against the wall in search of clarity. And stop looking for the *why* and start looking for the *good* in good-bye—because it's there. When things end with no warning and leave you feeling as though your world has been flipped upside down, something greater is at work. The exit of that person, thing, or dream was a boarding pass to somewhere new, somewhere better, somewhere you need to be that you weren't going to reach without losing some of the baggage. Realize that if a door closed, it's because what was behind it wasn't meant for you.

For something new to arrive, something old has to go. Every good-bye introduces us to our next hello.

Every time you release your hold on what is old, you issue an invitation to God to fill up that space with something new. The place you were might've been great, but it can't hold a candle to where you can go.

The only way to move forward is to let go of

everything in your life that has passed its expiration date. What am I talking about?

- ♡ Grievances—let go of anger, unforgiveness, and bitterness.
- ♡ People—exes and unhealthy friendships need to be left in the past.
- ♡ Heartbreaks—don't just let go of the people. Let go of the heartbreak they caused and the idea that you could have done something different to make them stay.
- ♡ Mind-sets—it's time to move beyond insecurity, fear, and worry.
- ♡ Plans—sometimes we have to release *our* plans to realize *God's* greater purpose!

These things might have been beneficial in chapter one of your life, but their time is over. A new story can only be written to the degree that you are willing to close the book on the past. And as comforting as the familiar can be, there is no greatness in security.

Whatever or whomever you're called to let go of, thank God that He meddled before you settled. And send a thank-you to whatever or whomever gave you the gift of good-bye because they unknowingly gave you wings to fly.

Every Season
Has a Reason

A certain melancholy always comes with the changing of seasons. Lazy summer nights turn into brisk fall evenings, cool fall breezes are replaced by the falling snow, and the never-ending winter suddenly reveals that it does, in fact, have an expiration date. And the season that changed your life in so many ways falls away with the leaves on the trees and becomes just another memory to keep you warm on a cold winter's night.

Typically, when Mother Nature shifts from one season to the next, we notice a visceral shift in our own lives, nudging us gently from one era to another, urging us always to reach for the next level and refuse to remain stagnant. I think God created the seasons as a gentle reminder that nothing in life is permanent: not joy, not pain, not friendship, and sometimes not even love.

I've learned that you can't force someone to be in your life, no matter how badly you might want him or her there. Things change. People change. Feelings change. You can either cling to the past and miss out on the future or accept the circumstances as they are, roll with the punches, and say good-bye to anything or anyone that no longer has a place in your life.

Seasons of life are gifts
from God that last
as long as they are
meant to last and not
one moment longer.

Remember, even seasonal situations can bring with them lessons that last a lifetime. If the love doesn't last, it prepares you for the one that will. If the limb you're standing on breaks, it is teaching you how to fly. If the career path ends, inexplicably and without warning, it's nudging you toward your greater purpose.

Seasons come, seasons go, seasons change, but the lessons remain. You can't force a season to last if its time has passed. Happiness is loving every season for different reasons. Embrace the season you're in, and when it's time to let go, embrace your chance to begin again.

Single Again?
Carpe Diem!

The Single Woman Says:

Singleness is an opportunity to live life
on your own terms and not apologize.

*S*ingle again. Two words that to some rival *stomach flu* or *dentist appointment* as the two most dreaded words in the English language. I have several friends and readers who are currently just starting to navigate, or renavigate, as the case may be, the waters of singledom after breakups, divorces, or other partings of ways. And it hasn't been too long since I myself was reintroduced to single life following the crash-and-burn ending of my last serious relationship a few years ago. So I know that this "Brave New World, Population One" of single life can be a scary place to be. But you know what? It can also be a really exciting place to be. It's you on your own with arms free to embrace the world and all its opportunities and possibilities.

When my boyfriend and I broke up a few years ago, even though it was my decision, for the first few weeks, I felt so empty. My schedule felt empty. My heart felt empty. My *life* felt empty. But I gave it time and started to rebuild my life, one brick at a time, and you know what happened? I woke up one morning, and it hurt a little bit less. And the next day, even less. Then one day it stopped hurting altogether. Over the next few years, I chased dreams and had adventures and restored relationships far beyond anything I could have ever imagined would be possible for my life. I saw a counselor. I found healing. But most of all, I restored the relationship with *myself*, one that had been sorely lacking. And I started to see with new eyes the flip side of "empty," which was space to fill up my life with whatever I wanted! And that's only the beginning. . . .

Benefits of Being Single Again

♡ *Single again* is a new calendar with endless potential. You're free to fill it up with things that interest you, excite you, and move you.

♡ It's the rare chance to get to be selfish—to spend uninhibited amounts of time chasing your own dreams, goals, and passions without asking anyone's permission.

♡ It means having two open hands, an open heart, wide-open eyes, and an uncluttered mind for inviting blessings, joys, lessons, and laughter to fill your soul.

♡ Basically, in the single girl's dictionary, *single again* is synonymous with several other two-word combos: *next chapter, blank slate, fresh start, new beginning.*

So what are you waiting for, Miss Single Again? Here are two more words for you: *carpe diem*!

Being single means
you are brave enough
to face the glorious
unknown of the
unaccompanied
journey.

Breakup or Break-Over?

One of the best times for figuring out
who you are and what you really want
out of life is right after a breakup.

They say there's a thin line between love and hate.
Well, I say there's a thin line between joy and heartbreak. Anytime something so earth-shattering in
your life happens that it breaks your heart, it also
leaves the doorway of your soul open to new emotions and new mind-sets that can shake, rattle, and
roll you right up to the next level.

Leaving the comfortable shell of a long-term
relationship is one of the scariest things a person

can do, but think about it: What would happen to the butterfly if she refused to exit her cocoon? She would never grow, never change, never acquire her wings. If you outgrew a dress, no matter how fabulously it once fit you, you wouldn't keep wearing it, would you? Then why are we so willing to stay stuck in a relationship once it has become clear that the other person is not our perfect fit?

Breakups have a way of shaking us awake and helping us see what we really want versus what we are willing to settle for. There will come a day when you will look back and thank God that certain people or opportunities were removed from your life because you would have never found yourself if you hadn't lost them. Consider this: if I had never gone through the messy, heart-wrenching, *major* breakup I went through a few years ago, I wouldn't have started The Single Woman. I might have married the guy I was with and been living "unhappily ever after" right now. You wouldn't be reading this book! It took the biggest crash and burn of my life for the *me* I was meant to become to rise from the ashes and inspire *you* to become the you that *you* are meant to become! How's that for turning a breakup into a break-over?

Realize that everything and everyone that walks away from you does so because they are no longer a part of your story. Be thankful that they were a part of your life, but be just as thankful to tell them good-bye. Nothing is as powerful a motivator as coming face-to-face with *good-bye*. And nothing is as beautiful as the girl who, with a broken wing, still flies.

If you are currently going through a heartbreak, a breakup, or a transition from two birds of a feather to flying solo, know that happiness lies on the other side of *good-bye*. That's what the sad movies and songs forget to tell you. After the pain comes the rain, and after the rain comes the sun! Before you know it, everything's coming up daisies again.

The funny thing about endings is that you will never have an ending that is not immediately followed by a new beginning. Isn't that a wonderful thought? Think about it. At every juncture in life, when one thing ends, another begins. And we often enter our new beginning through a door that we never could have pushed open as long as our hands were still filled with yesterday!

Remember, on the other side of that broken heart is a brand-new start. Right now, this very moment, is a defining moment in your life, so face it. Embrace it. Watch your wounds turn into wisdom and your trials turn into treasure.

It takes a heartbreak to shake us awake and help us see we are worth so much more than we're settling for.

Eliminating the Toxins

The Single Woman Says:

Toxic people will pollute everything
around them. Don't hesitate. Fumigate.

Into everyone's life, occasionally a little crazy must fall. It's kind of an inevitability, like hitting every green light on the way to work when you're trying to put on your makeup. You enter into what you are fully expecting to be a long-term, successful relationship, but because of your naïveté, trust, or purity of heart, you somehow miss the person's warning label emblazoned on his chest. The one that screams, "Beware! Toxic person!"

When you have a light that shines brightly, you're

going to attract a lot of, well, moths. But these moths will do nothing but dull your shine, get in the way of where you're going, and ultimately create a big ole mess. It is necessary, and even vital, to set standards for your life and the people you allow in it. Although it's tempting to enter into a relationship thinking we can change someone, more often than not, dating an unhealthy person ends up changing *us*. And not for the better. The truth is, your life can't rise any higher than your relationships. If you consistently date people who drag you down, depress you, use you, and betray you, those relationships, and your life, have nowhere to go but down.

Choose your company wisely. If you invite crazy in, you can't get mad when it won't leave! Unhappy people will go out of their way to make sure everyone around them is unhappy too. Don't fall for it. This is your party. You get to decide when to stop the music.

I once dated this guy who seemed like a good guy on the outside. He actually looked a bit like James Dean, which probably made it easier to overlook any early warning signs of impending craziness. (C'mon, now. You and I both know that I'm not the first girl to fall for a pretty wrapping paper without taking time to see what the wrapping paper concealed.) A few weeks into dating him, we were sitting at his house one night watching music videos. A Keith Urban video came on, and I commented on how I had once interviewed Keith on the red carpet when I worked for CMT and how he was a super nice guy. I might have also said something about how cute I thought he was. I mean, we were watching a music video. It's not like I was going to jump through the TV screen and ride off into the sunset with Keith.

Well, my James Dean lookalike became so enraged at my comments that you would have thought Keith had turned around in the middle of his video and proposed marriage to me through the television screen. It was madness. James Dean berated me for fifteen minutes about my terrible, awful deed of finding another man attractive. A famous man, whom I would likely never lay eyes on in person again. (I mean, really . . . I had already met Keith once, and lightning doesn't tend to strike twice.) My point is, Keith Urban was clearly no threat to my relationship with James Dean, yet James Dean was so insecure that he apparently wanted me to gouge my eyes out so I couldn't so much as glance at another guy. And this was after dating for only a few weeks. Needless to say, the relationship ended shortly thereafter but not before a few more insanely inappropriate outbursts from James. (I very appropriately blasted the song "Stupid Boy" by Keith Urban as loud as it would go the day *that* relationship ended.)

Remember this: it's not your job to cater to anyone's insecurity or to fix anyone's unhappiness. Refuse to jump on the Crazy Train, no matter how convincing (or attractive) the conductor might be. You can't fix or repair or save toxic people. They have to want it for themselves. Consider this: when you allow unhealthy foods to sneak into your diet, it seems like the greatest thing in the world . . . until it starts to cause massive stomach problems, breakouts, and weight gain. Allowing unhealthy people into your life is the same way. It may not cause much of a ripple at first. In fact, you might even have a great time for a while. Then one day you'll look up and realize that instead of bringing them up to your level of healthiness, they've dragged you down to their level of dysfunction. And it's just not worth it. It's a lot harder to get someone out of your life than it is to let him in, so be selective. It's your life. It's your destiny. It's your party. And not just anyone deserves an invitation.

You Have to Grieve It to Leave It

The Single Woman Says:

You can't truly heal from a loss until you allow yourself to really feel the loss.

When we're going through a loss of any kind, the tendency of the world is to tell us, "Buck up," "Keep your chin up," "Dry those tears," and even, "Don't cry over anyone who wouldn't cry over you!"

But the truth is, it is healthy and necessary to grieve the loss of something or someone that mattered to you when it exits your life. You can't truly heal until you allow yourself to really feel the loss, experience the pain, and cry the tears that will cleanse your soul and water the seeds of your new beginning. I don't think anyone should wallow in self-pity and misery for extended periods of time. But once your world is shaken and someone or some-thing you cared about is taken, it's only normal to give yourself some time to sit with the loss, allow it to wash over you and through you, and accept the fact that a season of your life has passed. Then you can get up and get on with it. Don't listen to anyone who tells you that you're being weak when you are simply being human. Part of being strong is allowing yourself to be vulnerable, to let down the walls, and to cry tears of sorrow before looking ahead to your new tomorrow.

> True strength is knowing that you don't have to be strong every single second of the day.

We need to be ready to grieve all kinds of loss. It may sound strange, but when I left my job in public relations a few months ago, even though I was leaving it to start an exciting new adventure of being a full-time writer, I grieved. I was truly sad. I had been at my job for five years, my coworkers were like a family, and I had a sense of security. I was good at what I did. I knew exactly what every day was going to be like. And I had a reliable paycheck coming in twice a month, like clockwork. The idea of the unknown was absolutely terrifying to me. And I think that's often what makes it so hard for us to leave a comfortable, familiar relationship or situation—even though we know we've outgrown it, the thought of not knowing exactly what comes next is scary.

When I left my job, I recognized my feelings of grief and fear for what they were, and I allowed myself to feel them without judgment. You can do the same. Cry and shout and grieve and do everything you need to do to get the feelings out, and allow yourself to feel sad without trying to protect yourself from that sadness. It's real, and it needs to be experienced in order to properly close one chapter and move on to the next.

The thing or person or job you are walking away from mattered to you. You invested your time, your talents, your emotions, and your passion into something, and maybe you didn't get a return on your investment. Or maybe you did get a return, but just not enough of a return to stay in a place where you no longer belonged. Either way, you have every right to give yourself time to acknowledge the loss and come to terms with the new space in your life. You can't truly leave it until you allow yourself to grieve it. Give yourself that time. Only then will you be ready to stand up, brush yourself off, and leave the past behind.

Part Six

The Bigger Picture

Be Still

As women we tend to think life requires our relentless participation. We assume that in order for something to be done right, we have to do it ourselves. And as single women we tend to think God needs our help figuring out the master plan for our lives. I mean, there are a lot of details to sort out! But guess what? He doesn't need our help. He just needs us to show up, do what we can do, then let Him do what we can't.

I have a very funny Persian cat named Jeeves. (I know. You're like, "What does a *cat* have to do with God's plan for my life?" But trust me. I'm going somewhere with this.) He has a flat face and a permanent scowl and a one-of-a-kind personality, and I adore him endlessly. He also has some really funny habits, such as pulling his food bowl into the middle of the floor when he thinks he's running low on food. He can have an entire layer of food covering the bottom of his bowl, but if it's even a little low, he goes into a frenzy and pushes the bowl right into the middle of the room so there's no chance of me missing it. Then he starts his nervous prance around my feet. Wherever I go, there Jeeves is. The third and final signal that he's about to panic from thinking I'm going to fail to feed him is a persistent "MEOW . . . MEOW . . . MEOW" that is repeated over and over until I'm ready to take his bowl, and him, and toss them both out the window. (Just kidding. I would never.) And all this drama happens because he gets it in his head that I'm going to forget to feed him.

I've had Jeeves for three years. He's healthy, happy, and spoiled, and I have never forgotten to feed him. But even after years of being king of the hill, he still does the ceremonial dragging of the bowl. Granted, he's a cat and probably doesn't put a great deal of thought into his reasoning, but for argument's sake, let's compare my cat's nervous, distrustful behavior to our own lives.

Sometimes just
being still is the
quickest way
to get to your
destination.

How many times do we ask God for something and instead of just being still and waiting for the answer, we drag our proverbial bowls into the middle of the floor because we think He's not responding fast enough? Chances are, our lives are sailing along just fine. God hasn't failed us yet. We're still alive, healthy, breathing, fed, and clothed. Maybe we're not living lavishly, but we're *living*, which is a blessing in and of itself. And yet we fret and stew and stress and worry and panic and pace and doubt and fear. We pray for something, and instead of trusting that God hears us and will answer our prayers in His perfect timing in His perfect way, we drag the bowls of our dreams and hopes into the middle of the floor of our lives and start asking Him, "Why? Why? Why?" and "Are we there yet?" and "Are You even listening to me?"

So much about single life is walking through the dark and trusting God for the next step. We face a lot of unknowns on the solo journey—the cities we'll live in, our career paths, our future mates, our plans for children. It's a daily leap of faith. And because of this, I think God calls single people to a higher level of trust. The single season is our season of life to jump off the cliff without a net because we trust God to catch us before we get wet!

Sometimes we look so hard for clarity that we completely miss out on the fact that a great deal of the wildness and beauty of life is in the unknown. The space between the question and the answer is a place of endless possibilities. So relax, take a deep breath, let go of what you think is supposed to happen, and let the answers seek you!

Ever notice how when you go shopping not searching for anything in particular, you find more fabulous stuff than you know what to do with? Well, the more you go with the flow of life and surrender the outcome to God, and the less you seek constant clarity, the more you will find that fabulous things start to show up in your life.

So stop dragging your bowl into the middle of the floor, and allow God to fill you up with His perfect blessings in His perfect timing. Just *be still*. Trust. Let go. There will be a moment when the answers will come, and you will know what to do. In the meantime, boldly live with the questions.

You Are Loved

The Single Woman Says:

Don't ignore the love you do have in your
life by focusing on the love you don't have.

It's easy as single women to have moments when it
feels as if no one loves us.

We have friends and families who love us, of
course, but when everyone gets busy in their day-
to-day lives with their respective significant others,
life can feel a little like a game of musical chairs
where the music stops and everyone finds a seat
except for us. As women we tend to pour ourselves
and our hearts and our emotions into everything we
do, and when there's no one physically pouring that
same love, attention, and affection back into us, it

can leave us feeling pretty empty. I've been strug-gling with this a bit lately—not so much longing for a relationship or to be married (even though I hope for those things to happen for me eventually) but just missing the feeling of being loved. So the other night I said a prayer and asked God to rain down His love for me with a small gesture I could see and feel. Although I never doubt God's love for me, it's nice to have a tangible reminder.

Fast-forward to the day after I said that prayer. I was heading into Starbucks, and a timid-looking homeless man approached me and asked if I would buy him a coffee. I quickly agreed. Once inside, I helped the sweet homeless man pick out his drink and purchased it for him, not thinking much about it. Another man in front of me saw what I was doing, and he in turn purchased my Frappuccino and coffee cake! It was such a sweet, unexpected, heartwarming moment, and it wasn't until I got back home that I realized what had happened. I had asked for a physical gesture of God's love for me just the night before, and He answered my prayer! It might not seem like a huge, earth-shattering event to anyone else, but I believe God tends to show Himself the most clearly in the small, unassuming, humble moments. He is so good!

You are valuable. You are worthy. You are loved. Carry on.

I told you this little story to remind you that if you ever doubted you were loved, doubt no more. You don't need a romantic relationship in your life to have love in your life. Even if you don't believe in God, He loves you and believes in you. Demonstrations of His love are everywhere if you have eyes to see. And sometimes I think He's even closer to singles because we are going at this thing alone. So keep your head up, your faith strong, and your eyes open for the little miracles all around you . . . because they are there, just waiting to be discovered.

Weakness or Uniqueness?

The Single Woman Says:

God can turn your biggest flaws into
your biggest cause. (He did it for me.)

*C*onfession time.

I've always felt that one of my biggest weaknesses was my tendency to be somewhat romantically challenged. I mean, let's face it: I haven't had the best of luck in the area of love. My romantic "roads not taken" include a wide array of generally un-datable and emotionally unavailable guys. From guys who stood me up to guys who hit me up for money at the end of the date and everything in between, I have yet to find one toad that was anything more than just a toad. But would I take any part of it back?

No.

"Why?" you're probably asking. Well, if I hadn't had so many insanely off-the-wall and wildly colorful experiences in love and in life, I wouldn't have a single thing to write about, and you probably wouldn't be reading this book right now. Every single test I've endured created my testimony. I might not have found love (yet), but I did find my purpose. I found my destiny. I found my calling in life, which is inspiring other single women like me. All because I chose to flip the script and look at my biggest weakness as my biggest uniqueness.

So now I ask you: What do you view as your biggest challenge? Perhaps you have always struggled with your weight. Maybe you're a klutz. Perhaps you have acne or frizzy hair, or you're painfully shy, which leads to social awkwardness. Or maybe it's something more serious, like an eating disorder, an addiction, or a health issue. Whatever it may be, know this: your flaws will always point you to your cause.

I'm not saying you deserve to endure pain or that your situation isn't difficult, horrible, and heartbreaking. What I'm saying is that in the midst of that struggle lies your ability to help other people through theirs. The burden you carry gives you the innate ability to help lighten the load for others. And your darkest, most pitch-black night allows you to point others to their light. Don't deny your weakness; embrace it as your uniqueness. Realize that it gives you a sphere of influence and a platform that you would never have otherwise. You have the ability to reach people on their level, right where they are, in a way that no one else on this earth can. Don't run from it; run toward it. And the next time someone tells you that your imperfections make you weak, say, "Nope. They make me unique."

Your message,
your ministry, and
your influence
are built from
your flaws. People
relate to humanity,
not perfection.

The Bigger Picture

There are no accidents. You
are here by design. Trust in the
significance of your destiny.

*Y*ou are here for a reason. There is nothing accidental about you. There is a specific purpose,
assignment, and mission on earth that only you can
fulfill. Never doubt your specialness. Even on days
when you can't see an end in sight and the light at
the end of the tunnel seems more like a faint spark,
press on through the dark. Trust in your destiny. It is
calling you, beckoning you, waiting for you . . . even
when you can't yet see it.

Your identity was decided long before you were

ever born by a God who is daily placing new desires and hopes and dreams into your heart. Your heart is the foundation of everything that makes you *you* and is the clearest signal you'll ever receive about your destiny, your purpose, your calling. To identify who you are, you must first identify what you love. For example, I have loved to read and write since I was a little girl. In fact, I was the first person in my first-grade class to take home a book and read it. It was called *Peppermint Fences*. How do I remember the name of the book today, at age thirty-four? Because it was the first thing I was ever passionate about, and it set the course for the rest of my life. So if you want to figure out what you're here to do, you've got to first figure out:

Who Am I at Heart?

- ♡ What is the first thing I ever really loved to do?
- ♡ What am I passionate about today?
- ♡ What gets my heart racing, my blood pumping, my imagination stimulated?
- ♡ What unique traits do I possess that align with the desires of my heart?
- ♡ What am I really good at?

Realize that absolutely nothing about you is accidental or coincidental. When you step back and gaze upon where your passion and your personality intersect, therein lies your purpose.

> Even when things happen
> that you don't understand,
> believe in the wisdom
> of a divine plan.

Underneath all the thousands of seemingly insignificant decisions we make every single day, something bigger is at work, something pushing us toward our destiny. There is a divine plan for our lives. God knows who we are, where we're meant to be, and how to get us there. He knew when I started reading *Peppermint Fences* at age five that reading and writing would be an integral part of my life from that point forward. It's easy to become discouraged when we stumble, take a wrong turn, or miss out on what looked like an amazing opportunity. But what if—just what if—there's a reason for all of it? What if that stumble prevented an even bigger fall? What if that wrong turn took us to the right place? And what if that opportunity was meant to be missed so we could seize an even better one?

Just like a puzzle, it takes time for all of the pieces of your life to come together. But when you dwell in possibility, you know that unseen forces are working to turn all those jumbled pieces into a beautiful masterpiece. Trust that in the end it all works together for your good, even when you can't see it at the time. And although you may not get there today, or even tomorrow, you will get there.

So keep hoping, keep believing, keep trusting, and know that every step you take, no matter how small, is one step closer to becoming the person you are meant to be.

Faith over Fear

The Single Woman Says:

Refuse to let fear rule the day. Feel
the fear, and do it anyway!

*Y*ou know those days when it's pouring rain with no apparent end in sight, everything looks gray and hazy, and visibility on the roadways is slim to none? Even with the windshield wipers on, there's always that moment between swipes when rain pelts onto the window and your vision is impaired, causing you to feel off-kilter, blindsided, uncertain, even fearful. All you can do in that moment is take a deep breath, buckle up, and forge slowly and safely ahead, trusting that you are on the right path even if you can't see the road signs that will tell you where to go next.

If fear is rain that patters onto your window,

blocking your ability to see all the great stuff ahead of you, then faith is the windshield wipers on the highway of life. There will be moments when you're not going to know what's coming next. There won't be signs pointing you to your destination, and the clouds of life will open up and pour buckets of rain onto the sunny day of your dreams. But if you forge ahead in faith, keeping your eye on the prize, eventually the windshield wipers will kick in, and things will become clear. That's the thing about fear. It can only hang around until faith enters the room; then it's forced to flee.

The flip side of fear is it forces courage to step up to the plate. Courage knows that it's okay to be scared. Being scared means you're about to do something really brave, something others might laugh at, scoff at, or judge you for. It means you're stepping outside your comfort zone. Being scared means you're taking a deep breath and facing the fear; you're taking the leap and trusting the net to appear.

Whatever you're facing in your life—a test, a heartbreak, a detour, a letdown, a doctor's appointment, a delayed dream—when the rains of fear come, let your windshield wipers of faith answer. Stand strong, knowing that your destination is still there. It hasn't changed, and it can never be erased by a few drops of rain.

A storm can
wash away a lot
of things, but it
can't wash away
your faith.

The Art of Waiting

The Single Woman Says:

What we are waiting for is not as important as what happens to us while we are waiting. Trust the process.

Waiting.

Arguably one of the most difficult concepts in life for us to grasp is the art of waiting patiently. Our instinct is to try, to strive, to work, to plan, to do everything in our power to inspire some sort of *action*. But sometimes what we learn and who we become in the process of waiting is even more important than what we're waiting on.

In my own life, I've certainly had seasons of waiting. I'm just coming out of one, actually, and I didn't do a very good job of it. Earlier I told you about how I left my full-time job to become a full-time writer, but that didn't happen overnight. As soon as I created The Single Woman Twitter page and started writing my blog, I knew it was going to change my life. When it really started to take off, I got offer after offer for a reality show, for a radio show, even to have a chocolate named after me! But nothing seemed like the right fit. And although I was chomping at the bit to leave my job for my dream, something had to pay the bills until I could launch my dream to the next level. So I hung in there. I kept writing and kept trusting and kept praying, and eventually God brought the right opportunity my way. But it took more than two years to get there, and boy, was I impatient at times! Like a kid on the way to Disney World, I kept asking, "Are we there yet?" But God was too busy teaching me how to wait to answer. Little did I know that He was using that waiting period to prepare me, to stretch my faith, to get me ready for everything that was coming next.

We're all waiting for something. An answer. A response. A reaction. A second chance. An e-mail. A phone call. The next step. A new job. A new love. A new beginning. I want to encourage you to embrace the art of waiting patiently. If you're still waiting for it, it means you're not yet ready for it, whatever "it" is, so stop looking at waiting as a punishment and start looking at it as preparation!

Ways to Deal with Seasons of Waiting

♡ Use your time between seasons as an opportunity to get good at something new or to get better at something you already know how to do. I continued strengthening the skill that I knew was going to play a big part in my ultimate destiny—my writing.

♡ Don't just stand still. Although I was technically waiting on God to show me my next big move, I didn't just sit there and wait on everything to come to me. I got out there and took meetings, sent in my manuscript to publishers, and kept up my daily blog and Twitter page. Although I didn't make any major moves without God's guidance, I still kept moving in the direction of my dream.

♡ Find a way to balance your dream and your responsibilities. Believe me; it's not an easy thing to do. I was essentially working two full-time jobs for about two years, but when you love something, you'll be willing to sacrifice a little comfort for it. Don't give up on your dream just because it's not paying the bills yet, and don't walk away from your job that pays the bills just because you have a dream. Work when you have to work; then dedicate a few hours each night to putting your dreams into action. All your hard work *will* eventually pay off, in one way or another.

The time between when you wish for something and when it actually comes true is a vital season. Sometimes the moments spent waiting for something are even more important than the moment the something actually happens. And not all wishes are meant to come true. Some wishes are only there to teach us how to wait. These wishes are no less magical; they may be even more so because they bring us not an instant blessing but a lifelong lesson.

During those seasons of waiting, remember this: The stretching of your faith is immediate pain that results in ultimate gain. It is in the waiting that we become who we are meant to be.

You're not just
waiting in vain.
There is a purpose
behind every delay.

For Every Good Friday, There's an Easter Sunday

The Single Woman Says:

If God requires us to surrender one dream, it may be because He wants to hand us a bigger and better one.

Several years ago, before I was The Single Woman, I was a television producer. TV was my great love, and it's what I went to school to do. I adored everything about it, knew inherently what it took to create a powerful and compelling television story, and refused to listen to anyone who told me I would never make it in the business. About three years into my TV run, however, I was devastated to be laid off from my job at Country Music Television as a result of budget cuts.

After that, it seemed my TV dreams were over. I applied for other television jobs, but nothing ever came of it. The industry in Nashville dried up quite a bit, and it became evident that it was time to release my television aspirations back to God and move on. So I did, trusting that if I was meant to be a part of the television world, God would find a way to reopen the door.

And reopen it He did. In April 2012, I was invited by Oprah's staff to be part of the VIP Press Corps that traveled with her to St. Louis and New York City as she taped *Oprah's Lifeclass* for OWN. Watching the show taped live, viewing the inner workings of the creation of the show, and meeting the panelists was a dream come true for someone with a producer's heart like me. And although I was required to let TV go many years ago, my willingness to do so without trying to cling to a season that had already passed put me in the position for that dream to be resurrected, bigger and better than anything that had come before.

Although my ultimate destination in life was

not to be a TV producer as I had once thought, I love how God still occasionally allows me to take little detours into the world of television production for no other reason, I am convinced, than to see me smile. I am equally thankful that He didn't allow me to cling to my own plans and settle for a career that wasn't meant for me. Instead He aligned my vision with His in a way that far exceeded even my greatest expectations.

> If God closes a door and a window, it might be time to build a whole new house.

I tell you this story to let you know that even the dreams you buried the deepest are capable of being resurrected in the grandest ways. Sometimes life requires us to surrender our plans so we can realize our greater purpose, but know this: from the dirt of our buried dreams can rise the most beautiful, un-expected, life-restoring flowers of our future. Never doubt or lose hope in the desires of your heart, even when they seem light-years away from coming true.

I urge you to resurrect those dreams that you buried long ago. Get back in touch with the brazenly optimistic part of yourself that got lost somewhere along the way. Begin to cry out to God about all those dreams you hold nearest and dearest to your heart; then sit back and watch as He finds a way to bring them back to life. A greater plan is at work. On the other side of every Good Friday surrender waits an Easter Sunday celebration.

Part Seven

Making a Difference

Be the Change

The Single Woman Says:

We are not on this earth just to stand still and look pretty. The museums already have enough statues.

It's not enough to talk about making a difference. It's time to get out there and actually do it. What can you do to make your corner of the world a better place? The great thing about the life of a single woman is we have a little more free time on our hands to get out there and volunteer, contribute, pay it forward, and make a difference because we don't have as many demands on our time as married women do. And is there any better investment in your own life than to make someone else's life a little better?

Remember: if you change *your* world, you change *the* world. If you ever doubted that one person has the power to change the world, just ask Rosa Parks. Or Anne Frank. Or Joan of Arc. Every person can do something. Start a committee. Sign a petition. Lend a hand. Give a hug. Love. The great equalizer is love. We don't all have the same gifts and talents to share with the world, but we can all *love*! Look around you. There are infinite opportunities to love and be loved. To give love, to speak love, to be love. You are robbing yourself of so many opportunities for joy in life if you convince yourself that the only way to know love is through a romantic relationship. You can change the world if you change *your* world, and you can start this very minute by shining your light as brightly as you can in your little corner of the earth.

Change starts with you. When you step up, you invite others to step up too.

Little Changes That Make a Big Difference

- ♡ Sign up to be a Big Sister.
- ♡ Volunteer at your local domestic violence shelter or homeless shelter.
- ♡ Consider going on a mission trip.
- ♡ Become a child advocate for children in the foster care system.
- ♡ Make a pact with yourself to commit at least one random act of kindness a week.

Several years ago when I was between jobs, the person in the car in front of me at the drive-through paid for my coffee and muffin. It was such a small gesture, but it had such a big impact on me. I was extremely short on cash because I was out of a job, and a stranger's kindness allowed me to save a few dollars toward my bills that I would have spent on coffee. It literally brought tears to my eyes. Now I make sure I do the same thing for the person in the drive-through line behind me at least once every few months. See how that one random act of kindness by a stranger all those years ago has been carried on and paid forward through me to others? No, it's not an earth-shattering act, and it's not achieving world peace or solving world hunger, but if it brings some cheer into the life of someone who may be in desperate need of a smile, isn't that enough?

Nothing is more beautiful than someone who goes out of her way to make life beautiful for others. You *can* make a difference. When you don't see the change, be the change instead.

Kindness Is a Calling

The way you treat people who are in no
position to help you, further you, or benefit
you reveals the true state of your heart.

When we were growing up, my sister and I brought home stray kitties and puppies that had missing fur, broken limbs, and in one case, a leg missing altogether. The animals that had absolutely no hope of ever being adopted and were one breath away from their last—those were the ones we loved the most. At school, I found myself often drawn to the outcasts. The little girl who had not one friend to her name I took under my wing. When the mean kids chased her on the playground, calling her names,

I grabbed her hand and helped her run for refuge. When the boy who always misbehaved in class (probably because he had absolutely no one at home showing him the right way to behave) was denied a treat at the end of the day, I gave him mine. Later in life, that same boy was killed in a drive-by shooting. It's entirely possible that he went through his entire life never being accepted or loved for who he was, and that to me is a true tragedy.

The Bible says, "Whatever you did for one of the least of these brothers and sisters of mine, you did for me" (Matthew 25:40 NIV). I interpret that to mean that God is paying close attention to how you treat those people in life who are weaker, meeker, and less fortunate than you. It takes such little effort on our part to make someone feel a little bit more loved, a little more accepted, a little more celebrated. Many races, religions, and groups of people are unfortunately treated as outcasts in our society. As human beings, it is our place to bring people in from the fringes and welcome them into the fold. All it takes is one look at Jesus and His band of misfit disciples to see a shining example of how to give meaning and hope and purpose to those whom society has collectively turned its back on. You never know the impact you are making on other people's lives just by showing them kindness and love. For them, you might be the difference between success and failure, holding on and giving up, and perhaps even life and death.

Take a moment to look around you and identify those in your workplace, in your church, at your gym, and on the street who don't quite fit in. Who better to identify with people looking for a place to belong than single women? It's easy sometimes to feel awkward and misplaced at social gatherings, family reunions, and even church social groups. The next time you see that girl at church cowering in the corner because she hasn't been to church in years and doesn't feel quite worthy to be there, it should be easy for you to give her a hug and welcome her into the fold!

Look around you for people to reach out to: The single mom in line in front of you at the grocery store who is a dollar short of buying food for her family. The older gentleman in your class who's working three jobs to put himself through school and finally get that degree. The recently divorced friend who has never felt more alone. Give them a smile, a hug, an encouraging word, a helping hand. There are many different callings in life, and kindness is one of them. Answer that call today, and give the person on the other end a little more hope.

Always show kindness and love to others. Your words might be filling the empty places in someone's heart.

The Gift of Love

The Single Woman Says:

There are no limits to what love can do.

We live in confusing times; there's no doubt about that. In the age of iPhones, iPads, iBooks, and iPods, the most important "i" of all—iLoveYou—can sometimes get lost in the shuffle. Instead of hugs, we send virtual smilies. Instead of calling one another, we send text messages. And instead of having actual face time, we have FaceTime. It's easy to get caught up in day-to-day living and lose sight of what's really important, but when all is said and done, when everything else goes away, when we're standing at the end of our lives, however long or short they may be, the only thing that really matters is love. The people we love, the ones who love us, the love and kindness and compassion we show others, and the goodness we sow back into the world.

When you get right down to it, many of the world's problems arise from someone, somewhere along the way, not being loved enough. Insecurity, anger, fear, self-loathing, jealousy, bitterness, even violence are the by-products of the love shortage our world is facing. But what can we do to help the problem?

We can do the thing that we were put here on this earth to do, the thing that human beings are uniquely built to do. We can love. We were given arms and tears and hearts and hands and emotions for a reason. God bestowed upon us the gifts of compassion, empathy, forgiveness, kindness, and mercy for such a time as this.

We can love—love bigger, love better, love harder. How?

- ♡ Replace bitter with sweet. Let some people off the hook—yes, even that ex-boyfriend who broke your heart. (Forgiveness doesn't mean you have to let him back into your life.)
- ♡ Realize that your best friend who keeps trying to set you up with her cousin's sister's

stepbrother is simply doing it out of love, and show her your gratitude instead of your attitude.

○ Show kindness to everyone you meet.

○ Tell the person you've been too terrified to be honest with how you feel about him or her. You have absolutely nothing to lose except fear.

○ Give your family extra hugs (yes, even the family members who drive you crazy). In the end, they're the only ones who matter.

○ Do the thing you've been putting off. Don't let something you meant to do become something you never did.

○ Tell someone who changed your life, "Thank you."

○ Pray for someone who wronged you. Be the bigger person—love your enemies.

○ Give others the gift of understanding, even if they don't deserve it.

We can love the hate right out of people. The gift of love is truly the gift that keeps on giving—giving life, giving hope, giving peace, giving restoration.

Love people who hate you. Pray for people who have wronged you. It won't just change their lives—it'll change yours.

Kind Women Versus Mean Girls

The Single Woman Says:

Mean girls go far in high school.
Kind women go far in life.

Lately mean girls have been everywhere I look. On my TV. At the movies. In the line in front of me at Forever 21. (Please try to refrain from making a "mean girl" comment to yourself about how a thirty-four-year-old like me perhaps shouldn't be shopping at Forever 21 in the first place.) And on my Twitter feed. Have you noticed some of the downright horrifying ways women attack each other on Twitter? People seem to turn into the grammar police—they never notice a single thing you tweet until you happen to misspell something or say *you're* when you meant to say *your*. (Not that I've ever done that, of course.)

No matter how positive of a person you are, someone negative is always going to come along and try to knock you down into the dirt. Sometimes we as women get a bad rap for being catty, petty, jealous, and just plain mean. We fight against this stereotype, and some of us even work to defeat this stereotype altogether, yet mean girls perfectly illustrate this stereotype and breathe new life into an old problem. Why must they always be on the attack?

It can be tempting sometimes, when sitting around with a group of girlfriends, to take off our kind-woman hats for a few minutes and engage in petty mean-girl gossip. But to do so is detrimental to our character. Instead of joining the fray, take a step back and look at the bigger picture. Mean girls often unleash streams of cruelty on women they've never met or know very little about. Kind women know that we are not Jesus and have not achieved perfection; thus we are in no position to be judging anyone. Mean girls think it makes them look prettier to call someone else ugly. Kind women know that it doesn't make us look bigger to make others look smaller.

You don't have to knock anyone off her game to win yours.

Ultimately, we are all a lot more alike than you might think at first glance. We are all struggling to fit in, to lose ten pounds, to cover up that embarrassing blemish, to smile from the right angle so that crooked tooth doesn't show, and to wear our most flattering pair of jeans, which might just be from Target instead of Nordstrom (but contrary to mean-girl opinion, the price tags on our outfits say nothing about our worth).

The bottom line: Don't be a mean girl. Remember that secure women don't feel the need to tear other women down. Try on compassion, grace, and kindness for size instead. They truly are one-size-fits-all qualities that flatter any shape. Give your fellow women a break or, better yet, a boost. Realize that we are all fighting the same battle, and if we join forces, we just might find victory.

Part Eight

The Single
Woman's Journey

It's Okay to Lose Your Way

The Single Woman Says:

Sometimes it takes a wrong turn
to get you to the right place.

I've never had a very good sense of direction. I've lived in the same town for most of my life, and I still manage to get lost on a fairly regular basis. When I'm traveling, I have to follow my GPS to the letter, or I could honestly be shooting for North Carolina and wind up in North Dakota. Once I was driving across Nashville to a friend's house on the outskirts of the city and found myself at the Alabama border before I realized I was lost. By the time I realized my error and got turned back around in the right direction, my friend was long asleep. What I did to get around before the age of GPS, I have no idea. But as someone who has spent a decent amount of time searching for my way back to Found, here is what I know: sometimes it takes getting it hopelessly wrong to find where you belong.

Although getting lost on the road isn't always much fun, getting lost in *life* can be the beginning of a grand new adventure!

- ♡ Getting lost in life allows you to see things you never would have seen had you not taken the wrong route.
- ♡ Getting lost opens your eyes to a whole new world outside your comfort zone. You learn that you are strong, you are capable, and you can take care of yourself and trust your instincts to find your way back.
- ♡ Getting lost connects you with people you might have never had the chance to meet had you not strayed from Easy Street onto the Road Not Taken.
- ♡ Getting lost shows you a side of yourself you might have never known existed otherwise.

The fact of the matter is, sometimes our lives have to veer wildly off course to get us to where we're meant to be. Sometimes it takes a detour we never would have chosen to take to get us to make a decision we need to make.

Sometimes when you lose your way, you find yourself.

So next time you find yourself alone out there, turn off your GPS and let your heart do the rest. On the journey of life, sometimes it takes losing our way to find ourselves.

Battle Marks and Beauty Scars

Anyone who doubts that every time we leave a place we leave a part of ourselves behind has obviously never moved. I recently moved, and as I stood in the doorway of my empty apartment the other night, I looked around at the remnants left behind once all the furniture was taken out: a hair tie, a program from church, a receipt from dinner several months ago with two of my best friends, one of whom has since moved to Los Angeles. Artifacts from the past year of my life, the last remaining evidence of an era that had ended. And even after I swept and vacuumed and scrubbed the apartment, signs that I had lived there still remained.

It struck me how much my empty apartment was a metaphor for life. People pass through our lives for days, months, years, or lifetimes, and they don't leave without making their mark. Sometimes it's a good mark. Sometimes it's a bad mark. Sometimes it's a little bit of both. Or sometimes it's your cat choosing to relieve himself in your storage bin of clean summer clothes that are ready to be packed away for winter. (Not that I'm bitter or anything.) But at the end of the day, no matter how much we might try to scrub our lives of any evidence of their existence, the impression of those people who have mattered in our lives remains.

And maybe that's okay.

Maybe instead of fighting it or running from it, we should lean into it. Maybe we can look at the indentions made on our lives by others as beauty marks instead of battle scars. And maybe we can let go of the person or love or friendship without letting go of the lesson.

This process is often sad, yes, but isn't that an amazing thing about life? The flip side of intense pain is intense joy. It made me sad to find the receipt that symbolized a dinner with a best friend who is no longer in my physical proximity, but at the same time, it made me smile to remember when he was. And that's what a good memory is made of: joy and pain, sunshine and rain.

Don't run from what was. Embrace it. Allow it to wash over you, cleansing you of the past and carrying you into the future. We're not meant to go through life as blank canvases. Things, people, and events leave their mark on you, and you leave your mark on them, resulting in the beautiful masterpiece of a well-lived life.

As messy, battle-scarred, and imperfect as your journey may be, it is uniquely yours, and that makes it beautiful.

Full-Circle Moments

The Single Woman Says:

When life brings you full circle, pay attention. There's a lesson there.

I often feel like the Queen of Full-Circle Moments. Sometimes the situations I find myself in almost defy explanation, like the time I discovered right before the photo shoot for the cover of my e-book that the girl doing my makeup was the very same girl my ex had cheated on me with. That was fun, sitting in the makeup chair for an hour in terror, expecting to look up when she was done to find Bozo the Clown staring back at me in the mirror. (Thankfully, she turned out to be very classy and actually did a great job on my makeup.) Yes, I frequently find myself back at a crossroads I've already crossed in my life, armed with time and grace and knowledge to make the right turn this time instead of the wrong one. Which then, of course, begs the question: was the first turn wrong when it ultimately taught me the lessons I needed to learn to make the right turn? I think all turns are right turns because if they don't take us to the destination, they prepare us for it.

Recently an ex's sister contacted me. And when I say "an ex," I really mean "*the* ex"—the one I struggled for years to let go of, the one I thought I'd never get over. His sister had been struggling with a broken heart of her own for the past few months and wanted my advice about how to let go and move on. I adore my ex's family and would do absolutely anything in the world for any of them, so of course I did what I could to impart some wisdom and guidance to her. I even shipped some books to her that have been beneficial to me in times of heartbreak. She walked away from our correspondence feeling stronger and braver, and you know the funny thing about it? So did I. It was a few days later that it hit me. The lessons I gleaned from the one man who had the power to shatter my heart into a million pieces gave me the knowledge I needed to help mend his little sister's broken heart.

What a beautiful full-circle moment.

There is value in everything you go through. Every single thing that happens to us, bad and good, gives us the capacity to reach people with whom we might have absolutely nothing else in common beyond our shared circumstances. If the tears I shed over my ex gave me the compassion, insight, and understanding to stop a few tears from falling from his sister's eyes—or my precious reader's eyes in the Philippines, or the eyes of the young lady who contacted me the other day from Malawi, or the single girl struggling to find her way after a breakup in some part of the world my toes have never touched—that is enough for me.

Wherever you are in your journey, I hope it involves a full-circle moment.

In heartbreak lies opportunity. Lessons learned from one broken heart have the power to heal thousands more.

The Upside of Tough Times

Nothing can happen *to* you that can't also happen *for* you . . . if you'll let it.

It's tempting when we're facing big challenges, changes, or consequences to blame someone else for our actions . . . or our inaction. "My parents didn't love me enough." "My ex cheated on me." "The kids in high school made fun of me." "My job doesn't pay me enough." At the end of the day, however, regardless of who did what to you in the past, the only person responsible for your present is you. When all is said and done, we all go through things in life that, if we allowed them to, could destroy us, make us jaded or bitter, or cause us to throw in the towel. But we can make the choice to let tough times polish us instead of demolish us, refine us and not define us.

The Upside of Tough Times

- ♡ Tough times help you prioritize your life, giving the right things more room and giving the wrong things the boot.
- ♡ Tough times teach you who your real friends are.
- ♡ Tough times remind you of how lucky you are to have the umbrella of faith to top you when the trials of life try to stop you.
- ♡ Tough times help you see the importance of self-love and self-care.
- ♡ Tough times stop you in your tracks, detouring you or rerouting you a different way altogether.
- ♡ Tough times shake you, but then they make you. Just as the oyster goes to great efforts to produce its tiny but shiny pearl, it takes big trials to produce bigger treasures.
- ♡ Tough times teach you that you are far stronger and better than anything that has ever happened to you.

Tough times inspire you to rise up and become the heroine instead of cowering down and playing the victim.

Take responsibility for your own life today. It's empowering. It's freeing. It's necessary for becoming who you were born to be. At some point in your life, you might have been victimized, but that doesn't have to make you a victim unless you let it. Allow everything you've been through to propel you toward everything you're going to be. Take your power back from the past and the people who hurt you by choosing to forgive and live. And stop looking for a hero and become one instead.

Life Doesn't Come with an Eraser, and Here's Why

The Single Woman Says:

Sometimes a mistake can end up being the best decision you ever make.

It struck me as I was walking on the beach recently how many different kinds of ways there are to erase things in life. You can clean your hard drive, wipe your cell phone, delete your Facebook page, use Wite-out on mistakes, and recall unread e-mails you sent in a cloud of emotion and bad judgment. Even the beach itself finds a way to auto-correct itself after a long day of kids playing in it and adults lying on it.

The high tide comes in and—*poof!* Sand castles and footprints and even items left behind suddenly find themselves swept off the shore. Yes, almost everything in life can be erased.

Except for life itself.

Think about it. If we were pencils with erasers firmly planted at the tops of our heads, we could say something silly or embarrassing and like magic, flip ourselves upside down and erase the words right out of thin air. If we initiated a breakup only to wake up the next day and regret it, we could recall our moment of snap judgment and the past twelve hours and be right back in a relationship. And if we made some horrible, foolish, unthinkable mistake that set our feet on a path we hadn't planned for, we could simply delete the mistake and be back to a clean slate. But although life offers many methods of erasing our many infractions, it doesn't have a method for erasing itself. Why is that?

I personally think it's God's way of encouraging us to live *big*—to take chances, to risk being nothing in order to be everything, to embrace life and its many fragilities and uncertainties with wide-open arms, to dare to step out on a limb even if we have no idea whether it can hold our weight. To do, to play, to see, to be, to laugh, to leap.

Focus on where you're going, but don't regret where you've been. There are no mistakes, only lessons.

Life wasn't meant to have an eraser. Much like enthusiastic kids, we're meant to finger-paint boldly on the canvas of life with no thought of how perfect the finished product might be. Life isn't meant to be lived perfectly but merely to be *lived*—boldly, wildly, beautifully, uncertainly, imperfectly, magically lived.

Notes from Life 101

The Single Woman Says:

In the middle of our struggle to find out who we are, there are infinite possibilities for beauty, hope, wonder, and love.

A big part of life is about learning lessons so we can become a blessing to others. As one single woman to another, here are a few of the most valuable lessons I've learned along the way in life, love, career, and friendship.

You might struggle a bit to find your footing in the career world. You probably won't get the big jobs and make the big money, at least not right away. You might have to start in menial jobs that force you to dress as a ridiculous wizard and stand in front of an apartment complex holding a sign that says, "Magical Move-In Specials" (or at least that's how some of us started out). You will probably get stepped on at some point. Someone you thought was your friend will prove to be less than loyal. You will get hurt, get fired, be underpaid, and be overworked. The good news is, along the way you'll meet people and have experiences that will make you come to life in ways you never thought possible. Every time you get knocked down, you'll grow stronger. And every time you refuse to get knocked down, you'll be introduced to a new side of yourself that you never knew existed. And whatever happens, you'll have friends there for you, either picking you up off the floor or standing, clapping, and watching you soar.

Things that once broke your heart will make you smile. Things that once upon a time you thought would kill you will heal you. Moments that used to seem like the most painful you would ever go through will stand as landmarks for the moments when your entire life changed. You will be able to look upon those times when you thought you'd never laugh again and be silently thankful for whoever or whatever it was that walked away—because without losing them, you would have never found yourself. You will, years from now, sit at a restaurant with your best friend and giggle for hours on end about the bad jobs, the even worse relationships, and the unanswered prayers that remained unanswered so you could answer the call of your true destiny. And you won't regret a single thing because every last bit of it made you who you are today.

You most likely won't remember everything you learned in school, at least not bookwise. You will, however, remember the moments that mattered the most: your first kiss, your first love, your first big heartbreak, the friends you lost (whether to death, circumstance, or distance). You'll remember the moments of sheer joy and beauty with your friends that would never be repeated once the veil of innocence was removed from your eyes. You'll remember the boys you pined for in high school or college (who've now gained forty pounds and subtracted lots of hair). You'll wonder what you ever saw in them and silently thank God they didn't share your affection way back when. You'll especially remember the moment you walked across the stage and accepted your diploma because it was the moment when not only your education but also your childhood ended.

You'll learn, as you get older, that rules are made

to be broken. Be bold enough to live life on your terms, and never apologize for it. Sometimes you just have to leap before you look and dance as though *everybody* is watching. Value the friends who have been there all along because when the others disappear and leave you heartbroken, those true friends will be the ones who are there to pick up the pieces.

> Ten years from now, make sure you can say that you chose your life. You didn't settle for it.

Dance. Smile. Giggle. Marvel. Trust. Imagine. Wish. Believe. Most of all, enjoy every moment of the journey, and appreciate where you are at this moment instead of always focusing on how far you have to go. None of us has "arrived." We're all still finding our paths in life. Some days are passes and other days are major fails, but at the end of the day, Life 101 is always worth it.

Epilogue

A Happy Ending? How About a Happy Life?

As little girls, we played with dolls and Easy-Bake Ovens, pushed our fake grocery carts around, and carried our fake purses. It was commonly regarded that the pinnacle of a woman's life was to achieve a Happy Ending—meaning marriage, kids, carpools, and white picket fences. We married off our Barbies to our Kens at age five, married off ourselves to our first boyfriends on the playground at age ten, and walked down the aisle to our varying Prince Charmings in our imaginations all through high school and college. Then we graduated from college and entered the Real World, and for most of us, that's when we took a look around, realized that "it is not good that man should be alone" (Genesis 2:18), and walked down the aisle toward our high school or college sweethearts

to live good, solid lives in our hometowns, get gro-
ceries every Monday, take little Suzie to ballet every
Wednesday, and have date night every Friday. And
there's absolutely nothing wrong with that.

Then there are those of us who entered the Real
World, took a good look around, and saw a world too
full of options and choices and dreams to pick just
one, a world that can only be tapped into while riding solo, a world in which one is company and two's
a crowd. We saw a world in which we live our lives
on the edge and have time to explore every last nook
and cranny of our hearts to figure out where they're
leading us next. We go to yoga every Monday, get a
manicure every Wednesday, and have girls' night out
every Friday. It's a world in which a Happy Ending
still feels like an ending and anything less than a
Happy Life feels like settling. And there's absolutely
nothing wrong with that.

> Some of us find love with our
> high school sweethearts, and
> some of us find love in our own
> reflections in the mirror, and
> despite what the world teaches
> us, neither is superior or inferior.

Some of us have the Bride Gene; others of us prefer Seven Jeans. Whichever way it falls, in the end, no matter how close to home you stay or how far you wander, the most important thing is coming home to yourself—being content to be exactly who you are in this very moment and realizing that a Happy Life has more to do with what's inside you than with who's traveling beside you. You've clicked your fabulous red stilettos together three times and finally understood that the power to decide what kind of life you are going to lead was always yours. It was always there. It never left. And it never depended on anyone else.

> You, alone, are already all the things you could ever hope to be: confident, happy, free, spirited, ambitious, determined, independent, strong, and most of all, brave.

You are brave enough to risk loving someone who might not love you back. Brave enough to go to dinner with two married couples and have a blast or to face dozens of blind dates in the hopes of finally finding The One. Brave enough to kill the spider or fix the leaky toilet all by yourself. To take yourself to a sold-out movie on a Friday night and smile the whole way through—not at the film, but at your independence—and to buy a house without having a clue what *escrow* means.

You're brave enough to love yourself just as fiercely as you would expect someone else to, and to proclaim that your life will be one of love and laughter, with or without Happily Ever After. You're brave enough to have the audacity to believe still that maybe, just maybe, someone at this very moment might be wishing on the same star as you are for someone just like you. But you're also brave enough to realize that even if he's not, and even if Prince Charming never comes along, just like the stars, you won't let being alone stop you from shining.

And most of all, you're brave enough to forgo a Happy Ending in favor of a Happy Life.

The Single Woman's Prayer

Dear God,

Thank You for loving me enough not to always answer my prayers in the way that I ask.

Thank You for teaching me that flying solo can create the strongest wings and that being a brave single girl is a beautiful thing.

Thank You for reminding me through my earthly father what a protective covering should really be and for giving me vision when I am blind and can't seem to see what's not good for me.

Thank You for showing me when I'm settling. And when I ignore You, thank You for meddling.

Thank You for sending me guys who didn't love me enough; they reminded me of what I'm worthy of. Thank You for standing back and allowing me to make my own mistakes and find my own way. And when I crashed and burned because it was the only way for me to learn, thanks for not saying, "I told you so."

Thank You for holding my hand even if I can't feel it. Thank You for collecting the pieces of my broken heart when I'm powerless to heal it. Thank You for being my strength when I can't be it. Thank You for guiding my path when it's dark and I can't see it.

Most of all, thank You for loving me enough to keep me to Yourself a little longer and for using my weakness to make others stronger. Amen.